Listening

Listening

ANNE LONG

Foreword by Gerard W. Hughes

daybreak
London

First published in 1990 by
Daybreak
Darton, Longman and Todd Ltd
89 Lillie Road, London SW6 1UD

British Library Cataloguing in Publication Data

Long, Anne
  Listening.
  1. Christian life. Listening
  I. Title
  248.4

  ISBN 0–232–51834–3

The scriptural quotations are taken from
the New International Version of the Bible
published by Hodder and Stoughton Ltd.
The poem 'Who Am I?' by Dietrich Bonhoeffer
is quoted from his *Letters and Papers from Prison*
by permission of SCM Press Ltd.

Phototypeset by Input Typesetting Ltd,
London SW19 8DR
Printed and bound in Great Britain by
Courier International Ltd, Tiptree, Essex

For
MARGARET
who has shown me
the depths of real listening

Contents

Foreword by Gerard W. Hughes   ix

Acknowledgements   xi

General Introduction   xiii

Section 1
Listening to Myself

	Introduction	3
1	The Story of My Life	7
2	Hearing Myself	11
3	How, When and Where?	20
4	The Value of Self-reflection	24
	Exercises	28

Section 2
Listening to Others

	Introduction	33
1	Listening as Ministry	35
2	Qualities in the Listener	39
3	What are we Listening to?	46
4	Some Cautions	51
5	The Process of Listening	55
6	Sensitive Areas	62
7	Resources for Listening	67
	Exercises	72

Section 3
Listening to the World

	Introduction	79
1	Listening to the Structures	86
2	Listening to the Nation	95
3	Listening to the World	104
4	Cosmic Listening	116
5	Listening to Paradox	126
	Exercises	131

Section 4
Listening to God

	Introduction	139
1	Listening in the Market Place	142
2	Listening in the Desert	149
3	Discerning God's Voice	157
4	Listening and Responding	166
5	A Listening God	175
	Exercises	181

Foreword

This is a timely book because its publication comes a month before the Decade of Evangelism, which begins in January 1991.

Many Christians feel ambivalent at the prospect of a decade of evangelism. For some it conjures up images of ten relentless years of earnest preachers, either raucous, or smooth, proclaiming the same message, or distortions of the message, from pulpits in churches, or at mass open-air gatherings, or on radio and TV, getting their audiences airborne in a transport of religious enthusiasm, then leaving them crash victims a few months later. If this proves a caricature rather than a reality, many will feel relieved.

Anne Long's book presents another understanding of evangelism, which we can all practise, a way of listening. We listen to the word of God in the Bible in order to recognise God now working in ourselves, in others and in all creation. The God of Abraham, Isaac and Jacob and Father of Our Lord Jesus Christ is God in whom all things live and move and have their being. If we listen, we can begin to recognise him in our hopes and fears, longings and desires, guilt and failures, in the lives of those around us, in our own nation and in our relations with other nations and with his creation.

'Listening', in Anne Long's sense, means being alert, observant, perceptive to what is going on within us and around us. In that sense, listening can be practised by the hard of hearing and the deaf, who are often the best listeners in that wider sense.

The book is easy to read, but listening is an art which we

can only acquire by practice, so there are many exercises suggested in each section of the book, exercises which open up all kinds of new possibilities for finding God, 'closer to us than we are to ourselves', a God who is constantly drawing us into unity with him, and therefore with ourselves and with all creation.

I hope readers will find this book as interesting and valuable as I have done.

GERARD W. HUGHES

Acknowledgements

So many people have influenced and contributed to this book, not only whilst it was being written but over many years, especially those who have taught me and those whose writings have enriched me. Many of the insights gained are theirs and, where possible, I have tried to acknowledge them. If any remain unacknowledged or their source not noted, then I apologise whilst also giving heartfelt thanks for so much that has become a deeply nourishing and sustaining part of my life. Ever since being on the receiving end of the pastoral care and listening of others, I have longed to hand on even a fraction of what I have received. With the invitation to write this book came the opportunity to do so. If some of its insights prove helpful to others, then I will be glad that what has been given so generously to me can be shared. The faults and shortcomings are all my own.

There are some, however, to whom I would like to give particular thanks. Bishop Morris Maddocks, Adviser on Healing to the Archbishops of Canterbury and York, and Anne, his wife, entrusted me with their vision for Christian Listeners and I thank them warmly for the many ways in which they have trusted and encouraged me since I joined their staff in 1985. I also thank Margaret Jones, Moy Gill and Sharon Stinson, friends and colleagues who have been closely alongside me with their prayers, insights and skills, and generous in giving all sorts of help and support. Also I thank my sister, Gillian Giles, whose warm-hearted encouragement helped me when I was flagging.

It was Dr Frank Lake who first opened to me the treasury

of listening skills and set me on the road of teaching others. He and Sylvia, his wife, listened to me on many occasions of inner darkness, as did Mary Freeman and Dr Marion Ashton, who helped me personally and have given us much help in the development of Christian Listeners. There has also been a group of friends and colleagues praying over a long period for the progress of this book, and I thank them for their faithful prayers. Others have contributed by sharing with me their own experiences so that these can be used as examples. Listening to them has enriched me. I am also grateful to Gerry Hughes SJ for the wisdom and insights he has shared which continue to enrich me, and to Walter Riggans, Christopher Wright and Ron Davies who have shared biblical and theological perspectives.

A special word of thanks goes to Joy Taylor who typed the manuscript. Her amazing patience, professional skills and constant support have proved a great gift and resource to me.

Lesley Riddle, previously of Darton, Longman and Todd, invited me to write and her enthusiasm was a great help in getting me started. When Morag Reeve took her place I found in her an editor who gave not only professional help but also care and prayer – especially when I nearly gave up! I thank her for holding me to the task.

ANNE LONG
Ascension Day 1990

General Introduction

Each day of our lives we find ourselves listening, but how much do we really hear? The day before I started this book was a good example – the early birds and lusty cockerel heralded the morning, the neighbour slammed his front door as he left for work and the Psalm for the day read, 'Listen my people and I will speak'. As I travelled to London I became aware of the chug of the train, the friendly laughter of a West Indian ticket collector, a strident ambulance siren, a committee discussion and, as I returned home, a tuning in to my own inner thoughts.

That evening the phone was busy – a teacher, tense and tired after a day spent listening to others; a doctor whose teenage daughter had been whisked into hospital with head pains and double vision; a woman recently bereaved of her father, whose husband was job hunting and who faced uprooting and change; a single woman, also recently bereaved, feeling the pain would never end and 'needing to know someone was there' . . .

At the end of the day I read, 'In Jesus Christ God took the whole human experience into his life. The Christian must be concerned about *whole* human beings and the effect that the *whole* of life in this world has upon them . . . '[1] Was I really concerned about them, I wondered – the neighbours, the ticket collector, the committee, the teacher, the doctor, the bereaved? How do you measure concern and where does it begin? In the heart? The mind? The will? Or perhaps the ears?

This book is about listening and learning to hear in the context of our daily lives. Other people's writings on the subject have greatly enriched my own learning and teaching. If this one adds to them so as to help people not only read about but move on in learning to listen and hear, then I shall be glad. For good listening is not as simple as it may seem.

To listen, according to the *Shorter Oxford Dictionary*, is to hear attentively, to give ear to, to make an effort to hear something. 'It is not a passive affair, a space when we don't happen to be doing or saying anything and are, therefore, automatically able to listen. It is a conscious, willed action, requiring alertness and vigilance, by which our whole attention is focussed and controlled. So it is difficult.'[2]

In each section I want to explore a different aspect of listening and hearing and its relevance to Christian living and pastoral ministry. To listen to myself may sound, to some, so egocentric that they don't want to read on! Yet it is only as I really listen to and hear myself and my own depths that I become more available to listen to and hear others. Certainly, to listen attentively to others and really hear them is one of the greatest gifts we can offer – a ministry in its own right. For this reason alone most of us need to discover how we can improve the quality of our listening. And it is as we learn to listen to and hear others that we also tune into the harmony and disharmony of the world of which we are part and in which we are called, in Christ's name, to help bring in God's Kingdom.' All of these sections are to do with prayer as well as care; that kind of prayer which listens as well as speaks to God. So, in the final section we look more closely at what it means to listen to God and to know him listening constantly to me, to us, to his world. Hopefully, the practical suggestions at the end of each section will be of use both to individuals and groups who want to practise and develop their listening.

One reason for writing about listening is, I suspect, autobiographical, for I sense I was a listener from a very early age. The middle child of three, I was an anxious and fearful little girl who often stood behind my mother's back, my face hidden in her skirt. But I listened, heard and absorbed a great deal – conversations, atmospheres, family ups and downs. I remember hearing the controlled fear in my mother's voice when, in the war years, the wail of an air raid siren announced another broken night. I remember standing on the edge of the playground watching and listening rather than joining in the games of the other children. Brought up in the flat countryside of Essex, I remember, as a teenager, my first visit to the Lake District hearing a whole new world of hills and mountains and lakes. In my first job, teaching English in a boarding school, I used to spend much time listening to the girls, especially those whose parents lived abroad and for whom the long Sundays were often filled with homesickness. Then at Gipsy Hill College of Education, I again spent hours listening to students, both on and off the record, in their training as teachers.

Soon after, I became a student again, this time of theology. I thought I had heard God telling me to go to Indonesia but gradually discovered that not every inner urge is the voice of God! I also discovered the gift of being listened to, when I suddenly plunged into a prolonged black tunnel of depression. Each night as I walked the dark streets of Marylebone I listened to menacing depths within me I had never heard before. It took time and painful attempts at trusting to learn how to share myself with Margaret, another student. The day she found me lower than low, and listened with sensitivity and respect as I tried to give voice to the pain within, I suddenly knew I had been heard to a depth I had never been heard before. The depression did not disappear – it has persisted intermittently ever since – but I knew from that day the priceless gift of being listened to and heard. I knew too that, even if I never got as far as Indonesia, the rest of my life would be concerned in some way or other with listening, not in a random way but as a ministry.

I returned to Gipsy Hill to teach Religious Studies, found myself increasingly caught up in the pastoral care of students and joined a Clinical Theology seminar group in pastoral counselling. As Dr Frank Lake and his tutors put us through our paces in listening skills a whole new world began to open up – a world of insights into myself and others where I started to see, albeit dimly, that personal pain could either cause me to become resentful or could, amazingly, become a resource for sitting alongside others who hurt. When Michael Green, then Principal of St John's College, Nottingham, asked me to join their staff and, amongst other subjects, teach pastoral care and counselling to ordinands with Frank Lake, I was ready for the challenge. I often wondered who was teaching whom, but it was an enormously rich eleven years.

During a sabbatical leave, I spent six weeks in North America teaching in churches and conferences and found myself listening and ministering to a whole spectrum of individuals in need. I was no psychologist, yet I had learnt something about listening and there were endless opportunities to do so. But it was exhausting as well as exhilarating – so much so that I wondered why I had been stupid enough to plan to stay the following six weeks in an Anglican convent in Hemel Hempstead, rather than go in search of a sunny desert island! Yet it was there that I learnt completely new things about listening prayer – it was one of the most important milestones in my life so far and was also to influence many of the students I taught in spirituality lectures. Numbers of them found their way to that convent and similar places for times of retreat and listening to God.

Three years later came another life-changing experience in an Urban Priority Area church in Netherley, Liverpool. As I began, under the guidance of the vicar, Clarry Hendrickse, to walk the streets and listen to the area – its badly constructed flats, lack of facilities, grey atmosphere and warm-hearted people – so I began to hear new and disquieting questions about equality and inequality, wealth and poverty, work and unemployment. There were equally disquieting questions about the Church too – how to help liberate people who believe they are at the bottom of the pile to receive and minister the new life of Christ; how to enable them to become salt and light in a poor environment; how to help them read the Bible when many of them are not bookish people. I recognised in myself the temptation to retreat into mother's skirt again, to flee back into a private pietism. But I would not have missed my time in Liverpool for anything. It made me realise that listening to society is, and should be, disquieting.

In 1985 Bishop Morris Maddocks, Adviser on Healing to the Archbishops of Canterbury and York, invited me to join him and his wife, Anne, in their work of encouraging the Church's ministry of healing. In particular, I was asked to develop a project called Christian Listeners – a training course for local church-based groups who would, by learning to listen to people and to God, become available to clergy, doctors, social workers and those in community care, for a simple ministry of listening. In preparation for the task and armed with a Bible and empty notebook, I went off to a convent in Kent and set about listening. Early one morning, as I tramped across frosty fields, a simple, clear picture of Christ came into my mind's eye. At first it seemed the sort of traditional face seen in many illustrated Bibles but, as I looked more closely, I saw something was wrong with the ears. They were small, withered looking, flopping down feebly rather than open and alert. 'And that,' God seemed to say, 'is what is often happening in my Church, the Body of my Son. I want people who will listen to each other, listen to their local community, listen to my world and listen to me. I want the ears of my Body to function properly.' A simple picture, yet one that continues to stay with me as relevant to the Church's mission today.

So a second and deeper reason for writing about listening is the conviction that the Church at the end of the twentieth century is facing huge challenges, some of which were accurately predicted by Alvin Toffler in *Future Shock – a study of mass bewilderment in the face of accelerated change*.[3] Amidst increasingly immediate, often heart-rending coverage of national and world affairs (the North/South divide, the nuclear threat, famine, AIDS, etc.), are we in the Church prepared to listen to today's world without losing hope? Even more important, are we prepared to listen individually and corporately to God who is Lord of the world, on these issues? 'We need men who can speak to the world about its problems and needs, not with worldly wisdom, but with a heavenly wisdom, bringing God's verdict and view to bear upon concrete situations, as the Old Testament prophets did in their day.'[4]

The third and most important reason for writing about listening is that it is central to the Bible and its teaching. Father, Son and Holy Spirit are in constant listening communion with each other (John 16:13f). God listens to his world (Psalm 10:17) and tells the world to listen to his Son (Matthew 17:5). Jesus' mission was a constant rhythm of turning in obedient listening to his Father (John 8:28) then turning with compassion to listen to people, not only to their words but into the depths of their being (John 2:25, Luke 7:39, 40).

We are told to consider ourselves (Romans 12:3), listening to our hearts (Psalm 4:4) and examining our ways (Lamentations 3:40). We are to be quick to listen to others (James 1:19), individually but also collectively, as we hear the voices of the world in which we live. It was in listening to his social context that Amos spoke out his powerful prophecies (Amos 2:6–8, 6:4–7). Above all and in all we are to listen for and discern the voice of God who longs to share himself and his ways with us (Jeremiah 6:10). As we find the courage to face into and listen with increasing discernment to what we hear, we shall also know in the depths of us that we are at all times listened to and heard by the God who made us, knows us and is committed to us (Psalm 139:1–4).

Of course, there are many disincentives to listening – the pace of life, busy timetables, our preoccupations – yet there is also a growing desire amongst many to learn. I see this reflected frequently in workshops and retreats. This desire both needs and deserves encouraging and channelling so that we can grow in this dimension of ministry. I do not intend to offer detailed instructions on how to listen – these are best learnt through experience and guided practice rather than through books – but I hope the principles I include will provide guidelines for fresh exploration. We urgently need, in these days, to become a listening Church. As we enter a decade of evangelism, if our activity is to be Spirit-directed and fruitful, we must first listen to what God is saying to us. No book can do that for us but perhaps, as we see the possibilities for listening in our everyday lives, we can become available to ourselves, to others, to God's world, and above all, to God himself in fresh ways so as to join with Christ in bringing in his Kingdom.

1. David Sheppard and Derek Worlock, *Better Together* (Hodder & Stoughton, 1988), p. 124.
2. Mother Mary Clare SLG, *Listening to God and Listening to Community* (SLG Press, 1978), p. 4.
3. Alvin Toffler, *Future Shock* (Bodley Head, 1970).
4. Michael Harper, *Let My People Grow* (Hodder & Stoughton, 1977) pp. 54–5.

Section 1

Listening to Myself

Introduction

'The unreflected life is not worth living'
(Socrates)

To think in terms of listening to myself in a world where millions starve, suffer from violence, homelessness and flooding might sound a strange pathway to either prayer or ministry. Yet the Bible provides clear pointers to listen to ourselves. The Psalmist wrote, 'When you are on your beds, search out your hearts and be silent' (Psalm 4:4). We are to 'examine our ways and test them' (Lamentations 3:40). Paul wrote, 'think of yourself with sober judgment' (Romans 12:3). When Jesus withdrew from the public eye to a quiet place, it is likely that he spent time in self-reflection as well as in prayer to his Father. 'He knew what was in man' and that was partly because he knew himself.

To grow in self-understanding involves becoming aware of what is happening within me at different levels of my being, learning to listen to myself. Inside each of us there are many and varied voices, some expressed, some known but unexpressed and some deeply repressed. Some voices we are happy to own (our achievements, satisfactions, joys, hopes) whilst others we would often prefer to disown (our fears, prejudices, guilts, jealousies). At times we can be uncomfortably aware of a confusing hubbub of voices within, all trying to speak at the same time. This is not just a twentieth century way of looking at things either. Richard III, in Shakespeare's play, wakes up in the night before the Battle of Bosworth Field with a nightmare:

> It is now dead midnight,
> Cold fearful drops stand on my trembling flesh
> What do I fear? Myself? There's none else by:
> Richard loves Richard; that is, I am I.
> Is there a murderer here? No – yes, I am:
> Then fly. What, from myself? Great reason why –
> Lest I lack revenge. What, myself upon myself!
> Alack, I love myself. Wherefore? For only good
> That I myself have done unto myself?
> Oh, no! Alas I rather hate myself!
> I am a villain; yet I lie, I am not!

'I am I', 'I am a villain', 'yet I lie, I am not', 'lest I lack revenge, What, myself upon myself! Alack, I love myself', 'Alas, I rather hate myself'. Mixed messages – yet most of us can, at least in part, identify with Richard in his confusion as to who he felt himself most genuinely to be.

Listening to my inner world is not necessarily comfortable yet it is as I dare to listen and hear that I gradually become aware of the different levels of identity and my continuing need for further integration and healing. And whilst the Holy Spirit is the agent of change, God still needs my active co-operation to bring about those changes that are for my growth and maturing. Moreover, and paradoxically, it is as I listen to and begin to understand the depths of myself that I become more not less available to others and their personal depths. Recognising some of my own contradictions makes me more open and compassionate to theirs. This struck me once when a student told me, with a broad smile, of his inner despair – 'the smiling depression' doctors call it. I had often used that particular defence myself when depressed and had experienced the loneliness of it.

Listening to myself is about listening to a story in the making – a story involving all the different parts of me and my life. It concerns the things that happen to me – outer events and activities – together with my inner perceptions – my thinking, beliefs and attitudes, my feelings, my relationships, my satisfactions and my needs, my past as well as my present.

Each day of my life I am making my own story. That story becomes immeasurably enriched as I learn to reflect on the different parts, for it is this interplay between the outer and the inner and my perceptions of it that comprise the uniqueness of my story. But won't this lead to self-centred introspection? Surely life is for living, not sitting around thinking about myself? Wrongly used, self-reflection can certainly become the kind of introspection that stunts Christian growth, causing some to spiral down into self-despair. Rightly used, it can become a creative means of growth into Christian maturity, making us more available to God and other people, for only what is recognised, accepted and owned by us can be given away. And it is very likely that, for every individual who pays too much attention to the inner life, there are another ten who do so too little, failing to develop that inwardness which is a preparation for action rather than an end in itself.

This is very different from the humanistic goal of 'self-realisation' or 'self-actualisation', frequent themes in contemporary humanistic psychology. For

> no amount of introspection, self-discovery, seeking for the buried parts of our experience can bring wholeness if we make diversity and discovery our ultimate values. There is a mysterious centre to our being, hard to describe or discuss, yet indispensable to our integrity. Modern man's greatest problem is that he has lost contact with this centre and he experiences overwhelming feelings of disintegration.[1]

Campbell describes this 'centre' in Thomas Merton's words as 'the inner sanctuary where self-awareness goes beyond analytical reflection, and opens out into . . . confrontation with . . . one who is more intimate to us than we are to ourselves'[2] – that is, God himself.

It is as we listen to ourselves in the context of the God who made us and knows us that we discover our deepest identity, not 'I alone' but 'I in him' and this is the Christian context we shall be exploring in this section.

1

The Story of My Life

Other people's stories have always fascinated me – not only the outward things that happen to them but also the inner movements of their thinking, feeling, spirit.

In AD 401 Augustine of Hippo, bishop and theologian, published his *Confessions*. This was a new kind of book – not simply a confession of past sins and newly found faith (though it was that) but a working out of his personal struggles, searching for significant patterns in his life, fashioning his own story. He constantly asked questions of himself – why was this so? Where was God when this happened? And yet, Rowan Williams points out, 'the question repeatedly modulates into a different key; not, Where was God? but, Where was I? "But where was I when I was seeking You? You were there in front of me, but I had wandered away from myself. And if I could not find my own self, how much less could I find You?" (V. 2)'[3] Augustine's *Confessions* are a profoundly theological example of a man struggling to listen to and understand himself in the light of the God who made and knew him.

C. S. Lewis described significant parts of his life story in *Surprised by Joy* and particularly his conversion. He was intently aware of his own inner self one day when, going up Headington Hill, Oxford, on the top of a bus,

> I became aware that I was holding something at bay, or shutting something out. Or, if you like, that I was wearing some stiff clothing, like corsets, or even a suit of armour, as if I were a lobster. I felt myself being, there and then, given a free choice. I could open the door or keep it shut; I could

unbuckle the armour or keep it on . . . I chose to open, to unbuckle, to loosen the rein.

He became aware too of new feelings within:

> I felt as if I were a man of snow at long last beginning to melt. The melting was starting in my back – drip – drip and presently trickle – trickle. I rather disliked the feeling.[4]

Momentous things were happening to him even though all an observer would have seen was a man on the top deck of a bus.

Dame Janet Baker decided to keep a journal of her last year as an opera singer before she retired. She wrote: 'I wanted to put one year of my life under a microscope, so to speak, because this particular year would be the last of its kind'. In the midst of very full days – rehearsals, performances, travel, planning, entertaining, public demand – she also made time to reflect on what was happening within,

> The years have taught me that the part of me which is a down-to-earth, Yorkshire working woman and the part of me which is an artist, can live together peaceably and enjoy all the different facets of this extraordinary life of mine; the battle has ceased to rage . . . There are indeed many diverse pieces of the jigsaw puzzle but I am beginning to see that they can fit into a pattern, and make up a coherent whole rather than tear me apart, making me feel as though I don't truly belong anywhere.[5]

Personal reflection, listening to the different and sometimes conflicting things within, is a way of laying hold of my life, living it to the full rather than simply letting it come and go unexamined. Henri Nouwen found, during his seven months' stay in a Trappist monastery, that he was learning a great deal about himself as well as about God (but then these are intimately linked). In the silence of the monastery he was able to hear himself more clearly. He realised how much his anger created 'restlessness, brooding, inner dispute and made prayer nearly impossible'. 'The most disturbing anger was the anger at myself for not responding properly, for not knowing how to express my disagreement . . . and for letting small and seemingly insignificant events have so much power over my emotional life.'[6] He goes on to describe the personal learning that went on for him. Rather than succumbing to unresolved inner conflict, he learnt how to listen to himself more honestly and learn new things which would affect his relationships with God and other people.

Gerard Hughes sj in *In Search of a Way* tells the story both of the outer journey when he spent ten weeks walking from Weybridge to Rome, and of his inner journey.

God speaks to us in the depths of our being, not off the top of our heads. The depths of ourselves are not in our reasoning and ideas. If we are to find God, we must learn to listen to these depths, to the emotions and feelings which we experience in prayer and out of it, and use our minds and intelligence to help us understand what these emotions and feelings are saying to us.[7]

These people's stories are all published but each of us is making our own story as we live out our days. It is made up of the outer and the inner, the ordinary and the extraordinary, the joyful and the painful. It includes all that happens to me and every part of me – my thinking, feelings, relationships, strengths, weaknesses, past and present. It is the story of my life. Hopefully, from the examples given, it is becoming clear that listening to myself and the growth in understanding that can come out of that, is not an invitation to self-centred living but rather the very opposite – an invitation to discover and live my life to the full in the context of the God who made me.

What prevents us from doing this? For some it may be over-busyness, letting our feet run our lives so that we never make time to become still and turn our attention inwards. Or it may be that we let our thinking dominate us at the expense of listening to our feelings, or vice versa. Some may fear what will surface from their own inner depths whilst others are unaware that one part of them, such as their body, is trying to communicate something important. Living in these ways is only half living. If 'the glory of God is a man fully alive' then this will include us being in touch with our own inner depths and listening to them. If we are out of touch with ourselves, not only will we miss out but so will others, for we shall be out of touch with them too. Esther de Waal aptly writes:

> No-one can be a good host who is not at home in his own house. Nor can I be a good host until I am rooted in my own centre. Then, and only then, have I something to give to others.[8]

2

Hearing Myself

How then do we begin to listen to ourselves and what do we listen to?

i. My daily life

This may sound very obvious since we have to pay attention to what happens to us each day. Or do we? Ironically, even with things we enjoy it is possible to 'have the experience but miss the meaning'. I often catch myself out thinking forward into the future rather than living in the present. It came as both discovery and discipline to read about 'the sacrament of the present moment'. Rather than live each day with only half an eye on what I was doing whilst already mentally moving on, I realised I needed to engage more fully with the present moment and let the present moment engage with me. In some ways this was easier with work but more difficult with other things. I remembered the wise words I had once heard that 'time is about depth rather than length, quality rather than quantity'. I started to attend to the 'less' important each day and soon discovered how much I had been missing. Sometimes I was deliberately attentive to the early morning – a thousand diamonds glinting on the dewy grass, a starling with a blue-green sheen on its feathers, the brilliant reds and pinks of the geraniums, the throaty call of the wood pigeon. Sometimes it was people whom my 'tunnel vision' had excluded – a lady on steel crutches shopping in the local supermarket, a plastic bag dangling from each crutch, yet with such a joyful face; an

African child with eyes like bright full moons; an architect deftly working on paper plans in a swaying train. Ordinary things, yet often bringing a richness to daily life that otherwise might have escaped me.

Jesus listened fully in everyday life – not only to people but also to his Father's world. 'Consider', he said, – or 'take note of' – the birds, the lilies, a fig tree, a mother hen and her chicks – for they can have a significance beyond the immediate. Michel Quoist, in his *Prayers of Life*, points out the significance of the commonplace, all around us if we will but look and listen – a telephone, a wire fence, posters, a tractor, a hospital, a bald head. 'The Father has put us into the world, not to walk through it with lowered eyes but to search for him through things, events, people.'[9] God is in all things and to miss out on the everyday may mean that we miss out on hearing him.

for reflection:
In what ways have I experienced a 'sacrament of the present moment' in the last day or two?

ii. *My thinking*

Part of our growth into Christian maturity is to become 'transformed by the renewing of your mind' (Romans 12:2). This mental transformation does not take place overnight. It requires patience, humility and a constant keeping company with the Christ of the Gospels. It will sometimes involve us in asking ourselves disquieting questions then letting those questions search us out. For example, what do I most deeply believe about God? Perhaps when it comes to it God is more of a policeman pursuing me than a loving Father.

'What do I most deeply believe about myself?' In asking a group of theological college students for quick responses to this question, an attractive, sophisticated girl replied 'A paper bag' – and burst into tears. Her inner emptiness was what struck her most forcibly about herself – the rest she saw as a veneer.

For her, the question became a gateway to personal growth and healing.

How do I nurture my thinking? What do I read? Which TV programmes do I watch? What effects do these have on my thinking?

for reflection:
In what ways am I developing/nurturing my thinking at present? Can I think of examples in the last week of how my thinking has been enlivened or deadened through conversation, TV, reading, listening, etc.?

iii. My feelings and moods

Emotional maturity is not about becoming dispassionate but rather living in the fullness of my God-given humanity, discovering and owning my emotions and learning to express and share them appropriately. The Psalmist is a good example of this, refreshingly honest about himself and his feelings: 'My soul is downcast within me'; 'My heart rejoices at your salvation'; 'Free me from my anguish'; 'Let vengeance be shown upon the nations'.

Awareness of my feelings helps me discover the colourful diversity of my personality. To be out of touch with them is like being oblivious to the full-orbed spectrum of colour in a rainbow. Most of us are comfortable to own feelings like joy, gratitude, love, even if learning to express them may not come as easily. But there is, especially among Christians, more ambivalence about owning feelings of fear, loneliness, anger, jealousy – let alone expressing them. It has taken me years to discover my own anger, such was my fear of it both in myself and in others. I frequently converted it into depression without realising what I was doing. With help, I began to discover both my anger and the energy it contained. Life began to be more colourful – and risky! Discovering our emotions is one thing, learning how to channel them is another, yet in the learning we become more human, growing into the likeness of the Christ who, in his earthly life, experienced the full spectrum of human emotions – compassion, love, joy, desire, indignation, anger, agitation, annoyance, dismay, dereliction.

for reflection:
As I read the feelings named in the last paragraph, which of them do I recognise in myself? Are there any I don't recognise in myself that I would like to experience?

iv. My attitudes

Attitudes are clearly linked with thinking and feeling but also with culture and upbringing. Listening to our attitudes and asking ourselves where they come from can bring to light some surprises as we realise how deep their roots go. This is, of itself, neither good nor bad. Rather, the question is, 'What are my current attitudes and how truly Christian are they?' Reading Richard Foster's book *Money, Sex and Power* helped me realise that my attitude to money was far more a reflection of my mother's than of biblical principle. Her constant fear was that we would 'not have enough to go round'. In fact she was a good housekeeper but it was her anxiety that predominated and which I unconsciously picked up. It has taken a long time to recognise the fear and its origin and begin to rediscover a more adult and biblical attitude. Perhaps a periodic review of some of our attitudes would lead to surprising discoveries and exciting growth! But this begins with a careful listening to ourselves.

for reflection:
What do I think or feel personally about my money? possessions? time? work? play? family? friendship?
    In what areas do I want/need to change?

v. My dreams

Our dreams contain far more than we often realise. 'We need to listen to them, for they are one of God's languages; vehicles of truth far too significant to be washed away in the flood of daily busy-ness.' Sister Margaret Magdalen writes of 'dreams in which God has revealed to me things I couldn't face in my waking moments – fears, resentments, jealousies, desires . . . but particularly fears.'[10]

It takes patience to learn the habit of briefly recording a dream then pondering it and seeking God's perspective on it. But in time this form of listening to ourselves can have a rich yield in terms of self-understanding and finding new ways forward. Sometimes, if I have felt low at the end of a day, I have asked God to shed light on things through a dream and what has come has provided ongoing food for thought, prayer and action for the next few weeks!

for reflection:
Can I remember a recent dream which told me something significant about myself? Am I open to hear more?

vi. My body

Our bodies speak to us if we will but listen, often telling us accurately what is going on at the level of spirit and feeling. A drooping posture can indicate sadness and heaviness of spirit, whereas an upright posture can indicate alertness. One depressed student who came regularly for counselling often sat in a downcast, sagging posture and for many sessions could not look at me but gazed at the carpet. Eye contact was too painful for some of the things he wanted to share. His body was communicating something important about how he felt. If my body is saying that I am carrying tension, anxiety, resentment, it is worth learning to listen to it.

for reflection:
Pause and listen to my body now – my breathing, posture,
comfort or discomfort – what is it telling me?

vii. My needs

Sometimes our needs present themselves in a clear-cut way, at
other times they are more subtle. I may have no difficulty in
knowing my need for sleep, food, exercise, but other needs go
deeper and may demand more careful listening. Personally, I
tend to keep my needs to myself and find it hard to ask for
help unless I know a person well. One night, after I had been
on my own for two days with 'flu, I dreamt of a large black
eagle who flew down through the trees into a forest clearing.
At first the group of people there (some of whom I recognised)
were slightly taken aback by the eagle's size, claws and beak.
As it approached them, apparently large and regal, it said, 'I
need your help – I have a wound'. They were surprised but
ready to do what they could, yet the eagle started backing away
from them. The dream gave me much to reflect on, including
my ambivalence about owning my need of others. Some important insights were given as I brought these to God.

There are certain needs which are part of being human and
the need to be in relationship is one of them. Jesus knew and
acknowledged that need and chose twelve very different men
to be with him each day. Three of these, Peter, James and
John, were particularly close to him, sharing in some of his
more intimate experiences, including the glory of his transfiguration and the agony of Gethsemane. He knew his need of
nourishment through friendship. He knew too his need of solitude in a ministry where people were always pressing upon
him. We all need both togetherness and solitude, times of
sharing and times alone, though the proportions will vary.

Our needs will also include a rhythm of work and play,
output and input, discovery of what sustains and what drains,
what we need for re-creation of body, mind and spirit. Knowing

our needs is a facet of knowing ourselves and we can grow in understanding as we learn how to listen to those needs, assess them and learn to live more creatively in the light of them.

for reflection:
What are some of my current needs? Are there any which represent an even deeper need? (e.g. overeating may indicate that a need for nourishment is being provided for in the wrong way.)

viii. My past

To speak of listening to my past may sound puzzling to some and unnecessary to others. Why dwell on what is past and behind us? Yet the Bible teaches the importance of remembering. In Deuteronomy chapter 8 the Israelites are repeatedly told to remember – to remember how, during the years of their wilderness wandering they had been protected, fed, clothed and guided by God. Such remembering would be a spur to gratitude.

But what about the painful memories, the mistakes, sins, times of hurting and being hurt by others? Surely it cannot help to brood over these? Yet the danger is that 'he who forgets the past is doomed to repeat it' (George Santayanna). The Christian is not locked into a fatalistic world of past guilt weighing him down and impeding progress in the present. Forgiveness is a reality but, more often than not, it involves the courage and humility to look at our past rather than pull the curtains across it. Facing hypocrisy can be the beginning of my own healing. 'There is no healing of the memory until the memory itself is exposed . . . as a wound, a loss. . . . The word of forgiveness is not audible to the one who has not "turned" to his or her past; and the degree to which an unreal or neutralised memory has come to dominate is the degree to which forgiveness is difficult.'[11]

To turn to our past, we may need the support of someone

who will be with us as we look again at the painful memory,
own it and seek God's saving action in it. And we will not be
disappointed for he is unconditionally for us, waiting to loose
us from what binds and burdens us, so that we can go on, not
having forgotten but having had the memory cleansed, forgiven, healed, transfigured.

for reflection:
In listening to my past, are there any particular memories which
are still spoiling my present and which await God's healing
touch?

ix. My relationships

We can never fully come to know ourselves in isolation but
only in the context of relationship. And this is one of the
greatest treasure stores we have. 'It is a law, as certain as the
law of gravity, that he who is understood and loved will grow
as a person; he who is estranged will die in his cell of solitary
confinement, alone.'[12]

. So it is worth reflecting on the relationships in my life, not so
much the quantity as the quality. Which are the most important
relationships in my life? What do I receive from them? What
do I put into them? How do I work at enriching them? In what
ways can I be destructive in relationships?

And what about relationship with myself? Jesus' words 'Love
your neighbour as [or, in the same way as] yourself', indicate
at least a self-acceptance which we sometimes find hard, and
at most, a recognition of the uniqueness and worth of the
person I am, seeing myself as God sees me. So as I listen to
myself, what do I hear? What do I like and dislike in myself?
How do I see my strengths and weaknesses? Am I held captive
by attitudes to myself which prevent me from growing into the
person God wants me to be? Are there censoring voices in me
telling me I'm 'no good', 'second rate', 'inferior'? In short, am
I learning to value myself? For it is as we grow into a right

recognition of our own worth that we also grow in recognising the worth of others.

What do we hear too about our relationship with God – not so much in terms of belief as quality of relationship? Do we feel close to or distant from him? Warm or cold? Do I bring to him every part of myself and my life or only 'Sunday best'? Do I relate more to God? Jesus? the Holy Spirit? With my mind chiefly, or my feelings or both? Do I prefer relating to God on my own or in a group? Do I prefer silent or verbal prayer? Set or extempore prayers? God has many more ways of coming to us than we often realise. Discovering we are in a rut rather than a growing relationship can help us reach out with a deeper desire.

for reflection:
As I reflect on my closest relationships (e.g. spouse, friend, child, colleague) what am I aware of in the light of some of the questions suggested above? Or did anything strike me as I read the questions about my relationship with God, or my feelings about myself?

3

How, When and Where?

Such ways of listening to ourselves are suggestions only, pointers to an increased self-awareness rather than an inventory to be worked through. But when and where can we listen to ourselves?

i. The 'little solitudes'

Lengthy periods for reflection are available to very few of us. But there are the 'little solitudes', brief moments when we can listen. It may be as we travel to work or after the family has gone out in the morning or in the lunch-hour or last thing at night. Perhaps there will be a specific starting-point, such as a feeling of joy or heaviness, a physical tension, an unfinished conversation, something that happened, a niggling question, etc. Let it surface, feel your feelings and discover more about what is happening within. Ask the Holy Spirit to give you his light.

Occasionally it may be possible to take longer times for this. Once a month, if possible, I spend most of a day at a nearby convent, primarily to listen to God and pray, but this often includes time for self-reflection. 'Why was my reaction to X so exaggerated?' 'Why am I so anxious about . . . ?' The insights that come have often led on to hearing God and fresh advances. Whatever the shortness or length of time available, solitude can become a 'furnace of transformation',[13] not always easy but enabling us to hear ourselves and God in fresh ways.

ii. Review of the day

'Without the discipline of self-examination we shall find ourselves battling against unseen and enervating forces in our efforts to do what we regard as our Christian duty.'[14]

As we learn to listen to ourselves, it can be helpful, at the end of a day, to review and offer it to God. Otherwise we are more likely to carry into the night what is unresolved, unconfessed and often enervating.

a. I ask for God's light (rather than my own) on the past day, that he will bring to my mind whatever he wants me to see.

b. I start looking back on the events of the day – things that have happened, people I have met, choices made, words spoken or left unspoken. I avoid self-judgments. What am I grateful for? I thank God for those things.

c. I recall my inner moods and feelings again, without judging them, and see what stands out – love, patience, joy, anxiety, pain, resentment, etc. I ask God to show me those attitudes and desires which were underlying my moods. Were they directed to his Kingdom or my own? I ask him to forgive me those times when I excluded him from my activities, relationships, words, moods, decisions. He never refuses to forgive us when we face up to ourselves honestly.

d. I entrust myself to God for the night and tomorrow, 'like a child in its mother's arms' (Psalm 131:2).

iii. Keeping a journal

A journal is for reflecting on the events, outer and inner, of everyday life. Morton Kelsey described what he found helpful in keeping one,

I make a point to write about my angers and fears and hurts, depressions and disappointments and anxieties, my joys and thanksgivings, my experiences of real fellowship and closeness. In short I set down the feelings and events that have mattered to me, high moments and low . . . The journal is like a little island of solid rock on which we can stand and see the waves and storms for what they really are.[15]

We can also record dreams, dialogue with people, work on problems through writing, explore choices, reflect on past events and memories so as to integrate them more fully into the present, recording also those things God is saying to us.

A journal is not an invitation to be unhelpfully introspective. Indeed it can become an important gateway to new understanding and growth. I find an ordinary spiral-bound lined notebook is easy to write in and can be carried around with me. Recently, after a group meeting that felt complex and confusing, I came away feeling hassled and angry. That evening I wrote out my feelings in as much detail as possible and found that God was pointing out other perspectives as well as my own which I needed to recognise. I explored these in writing until things began to make more sense. In that way there came fresh clarification and ways forward – and it only took twenty minutes.

iv. Sharing with others

One of the greatest riches we can have is trusted friends who care enough about our ongoing growth to help us stop hiding and face ourselves honestly. It may be in a one-to-one relationship or in a small group where anything can be freely said. Like many, I fear being criticised but can receive it far better when I know I am loved.

There are various ways in which this can happen – friendship that is free from collusion, spiritual direction (which need not be the authoritarian relationship the term may suggest), a peer group committed to each other's growth. One of the most important, though not always comfortable, places of growth for me over the past six years has been a group of eight of us who meet twice a year for a weekend. Individually and together, with the help of an experienced group leader, we explore aspects of ourselves where we need personal change and growth. Our times together have brought us very close and our commitment to each other's ongoing development is a high priority. We have learnt to share together, cry together, laugh and celebrate together, pray together and encourage each other forward on the path to maturity. We have discovered that honest sharing of ourselves in those areas where we need to change is no luxury – indeed it is vital and life-giving if we really want to grow.

C. S. Lewis once said that he would sometimes pray not for self-knowledge in general but 'just as much as I can bear – the little daily dose'. If we fear that what we hear as we listen to ourselves will overwhelm us, we can always take his advice and ask for the 'little daily dose'.

4

The Value of Self-reflection

So far we have considered different ways and contexts in which we can listen to ourselves and grow in self-understanding. What then is its value?

As we practise self-reflection so we become increasingly aware of God's hand upon us throughout our life. The Psalmist recalled with a sense of wonder that his actions, thoughts, moods, comings and goings, past and present were all known to God whose hand had been upon him from his earliest beginnings in the womb (Psalm 139). His own self-knowledge was held in the loving knowledge of God, so with confidence he could ask God to 'search me', 'test me', 'see me', 'lead me'. Henri Nouwen recognised God's touch upon him when he wrote in *The Genesee Diary*, 'I think that nothing is accidental but that God moulded me through the events of my life and that I am called to recognise his moulding hand and praise him in gratitude for the great things he has done to me'.[16]

But through self-reflection I also become aware of the great biblical themes being re-enacted in my own life – *my* creation, *my* redemption, *my* experiences of wilderness, temptation, deliverance, transfiguration, suffering, death, resurrection, pentecost. I am God's story continued. Again Henri Nouwen wrote, 'I wonder if I really have listened carefully enough to the God . . . of my history, and have recognised him when he called me by my name, broke the bread, or asked me to cast out my nets after a fruitless day?'[17] It may not, of course, always strike me like that at the time, and hence the importance of remembering. It has often been in retrospect that I have recognised a fresh invitation from God to walk on the water, do a bit more dying or receive a fresh glimpse of resurrection life.

It is in these experiences that there comes the opportunity for fresh growth. With reflection comes insight and with insight the chance to move forward in fresh directions with renewed hope. It happened to the Prodigal Son when he 'came to himself' in the far country and decided to return home to his father. And the good news of 'metanoia' (repentance) is that as we dare to turn and return, so we are led forward into Christ, the Way. This calls for courage, especially as we come face to face again with our own weaknesses, vulnerabilities, failures and sins. But the good news of 'metanoia' is that we cannot bring about in ourselves those changes that we desire. It is always gift and grace – Christ acting on and in us to create a new willingness to see with his eyes, hear with his ears, think with his mind and live out his life. 'Metanoia' is about transformation and God is both agent and goal. He does the transforming but our 'yes' is necessary, that daily 'yes' to the God who seeks to bring about in us those changes of thinking, feeling and living which will bring us to Christlikeness.

At the heart of listening to myself is an important question about stewardship of time, gifts, energies, relationships, 'What am I making out of what I have been given?' In the spirit of the parable of the talents (Matthew 25) it is helpful periodically to look at different areas of my life. It was whilst I was in Liverpool that I heard from Bishop David Sheppard of how he encouraged the clergy in his diocese to make an annual review as a way of standing back and looking at his/her Christian stewardship, then discussing these with someone else. It required listening to oneself. In time, our college staff at St John's, Nottingham, formed triads for personal review, mutual support and prayer, and most of us found these extremely helpful – especially the prayerful self-reflection done as preparation. True, there are aspects of our development where this kind of approach is problematic. Some genuine growth feels more like going backwards than forwards, down rather than up. But even in such times of darkness and discouragement, God is committed to us and our growth –

> A condition of complete simplicity
> (Costing not less than everything)[18]

In the end our personal growth is not just for ourselves but for others and for God himself. If I want to listen fully and compassionately to other people and their stories then I must do the same for myself, aware that 'the gift given me to give to the community is my *self*, ultimately; my story given back, to give me a place in the net of exchange, the web of gifts, which is Christ's Church'.[19]

And this is what Christianly lifts self-reflection and listening to myself to a dimension very different from 'self-realisation' and 'self-actualisation'. To see 'I-myself' as the goal is illusory. It is as we learn to listen to ourselves in relationship with our Maker that we will be given glimpses of our true selfhood, not 'I-myself' but 'I-in-him' for I am most fully myself when I find myself in God. This was the discovery Bonhoeffer made when he was in solitary confinement in prison:

> Who am I? They often tell me
> I would step from my cell's confinement
> calmly, cheerfully, firmly,
> like a squire from his country-house.

> Who am I? They often tell me
> I would talk to my warders
> freely and friendly and clearly,
> as though it were mine to command.

> Who am I? They also tell me
> I would bear the days of misfortune
> equably, smilingly, proudly,
> like one accustomed to win.

> Am I then really all that which
>   other men tell of?

Or am I only what I myself know of myself,
restless and longing and sick,
    like a bird in a cage,
struggling for breath,
as though hands were compressing my throat,
yearning for colours, for flowers,
    for the voices of birds,
thirsting for words of kindness,
    for neighbourliness,
tossing in expectation of great events,
powerlessly trembling for friends at
    an infinite distance,
weary and empty at praying,
    at thinking, at making,
faint, and ready to say farewell to it all?

Who am I? This or the other?
Am I one person today and tomorrow another?
Am I both at once? A Hypocrite before others,
and before myself a contemptibly
    woebegone weakling?
Or is something within me still
    like a beaten army,
fleeing in disorder from victory
    already achieved?

Who am I? They mock me,
    those lonely questions of mine,
Whoever I am,
    thou knowest, O God, I am thine![20]

Exercises

Chapter 1   The Story of My Life
1. What have been some of the important experiences of personal growth in my life – joyful and painful?
2. Who are some of the people through whom I have grown?
3. Where was God in the tough times?

Chapter 2   Hearing Myself
1. Spend time reflecting on some of the suggested questions. Is there one particular area where I need to listen to myself in more depth at present?
2. As I listen to myself in these different areas, is there anything that I want before I die? (e.g. an ambition I would like to fulfil? a relationship I would like to improve? etc.)

Chapter 3   How, When and Where?
1. Start keeping a personal journal. A simplified version could include:
    — daily causes for thanksgiving
    — notes about my spiritual journey, things that challenge me, concern me, strengthen me, etc.
    — something I am reading or thinking about at present that I would like to remember
    — a current event or relationship I want to reflect on
2. Use the nightly review (page 21) over the next week and see how I find it.

Chapter 4   The Value of Self-reflection
1. Make notes on my own Christian journey and what God has meant to me at different times in my life.

References

1. Alastair V. Campbell, *Rediscovering Pastoral Care* (DLT, 1981), p. 14.
2. Alastair Campbell quoting from Thomas Merton, *Contemplative Prayer* (DLT, 1973), p. 38.
3. Rowan Williams, *The Wound of Knowledge* (DLT, 1979), p. 68.
4. C. S. Lewis, *Surprised by Joy* (Fontana, 1959), p. 179.
5. Janet Baker, *Full Circle* (Julia MacRae, 1982), p. 122.
6. Henri Nouwen, *The Genesee Diary* (Doubleday Image Books, 1981), p. 44.
7. Gerard Hughes sj, *In Search of a Way* (DLT, 1986), p. 20.
8. Esther de Waal, *Living with Contradiction* (Collins Fount, 1989), p. 95.
9. Michel Quoist, *Prayers of Life* (Gill & Son, 1963), p. 14.
10. Ed. Edward England, *Keeping a Spiritual Journal* (Highland Books, 1988), pp. 73–4.
11. Rowan Williams, *Resurrection* (DLT, 1982), p. 21.
12. John Powell, *Why am I afraid to tell you who I am?* (Fontana, 1975), p. 96.
13. Henri Nouwen, *The Way of the Heart* (DLT, 1981), p. 25.
14. Alastair V. Campbell, *op. cit.,* p. 101.
15. Morton Kelsey, *The Other Side of Silence* (Paulist Press, 1976), p. 199.
16. Henri Nouwen, *The Genesee Diary*, p. 94.
17. *Ibid.*
18. T. S. Eliot, *Little Gidding – Four Quartets* (Faber & Faber, 1944), p. 44.
19. Rowan Williams, *Resurrection*, pp. 43–4.
20. Dietrich Bonhoeffer, *Letters and Papers from Prison* (SCM, 1967), p. 348.

Section 2

Listening to Others

Introduction

> The beginning of love for the brethren is learning to listen
> to them.
>
> (Bonhoeffer)

Elaine, a busy mother of four, had asked if she could come to
see me – she had been feeling unhappy recently. We spent time
together and two weeks later she returned for another hour of
sharing. When I asked her how she was feeling she replied,
'It's been like coming out of prison'. Being listened to and
heard can feel as liberating as that. I remember experiencing
it myself when, during a bad bout of depression, I falteringly
shared with Colin and Di my inner pain and darkness. Simple
listening presence is, I discovered, immensely comforting.
There are times when what we most need is not words of advice
or direction but the knowledge that someone is there, accepting
us as we are, that we are not after all alone.

It sounds simple and sometimes is, yet there is more to
listening than meets the eye. If some of the qualities needed
in a good listener come naturally, others do not and need to
be learnt and worked at. Even the born listener can refine and
improve his gift so that it becomes a deeper, richer ministry.
For listening is a multi-dimensional activity. Hearing the words
that someone speaks is to receive only one aspect of his communication. There are also other levels which need to be heard
and understood – his style of speaking, his feelings, thinking,
attitudes, body, silences. All these are dimensions of the person
which we must learn to hear if we are to understand him.

We need also to grow in self-awareness as to how we listen to
others. Do I interrupt too often? Do I ask helpful or unhelpful
questions? Do I jump in with my own story and take over? We
are often unaware of what in us can help or hinder the person
needing a listening ear. Moreover, listening does not stop at
listening. Where do I go with a person after I've listened?

'After all, you've got to have some answers to give people, haven't you?' said John as we were discussing the value of listening. Yes, but whose answers – the listener's? the speaker's? some of each? It is all too easy to jump in with suggestions, advice, solutions, and whilst there is certainly a place for advice-giving, it is far more important that a person discovers what *he* needs rather than be given someone else's answers which may turn out to be a bad fit.

Good listeners develop and grow by learning to reflect on the questions and difficulties that inevitably arise in the listening relationship. For example, what do I do when other people's confidences feel burdensome and start getting me down? Where do I turn when I reach the limits of my own competence in listening to certain areas of someone's life experience? How do I handle over-dependency? These and other questions can be uncomfortable reminders that, to be involved in a ministry of listening, we need personal and spiritual resources. In Jesus' ministry we see a rhythm of taking in and giving out. He was resourced by his friends, by food, sleep, exercise, the created world and, supremely, by spending time with his Father. Then he gave out to individuals and crowds in healing, casting out evil, teaching, encouraging, challenging. Having given out he would make space to take in again and become resourced (Mark 1:29–45). This rhythm of input and output characterised his daily living. Anyone involved in a ministry of listening will need to take Jesus' pattern seriously for only in this way will exhaustion and burnout be avoided. I find that when I take my own resourcing seriously I approach listening with a far greater sense of freshness and expectation that God will work, whereas when I don't I can feel reluctant, unexpectant and sometimes plain resentful.

These, then, are some aspects we shall consider as we think about listening to others.

1

Listening as Ministry

Counselling textbooks often refer to 'active listening' and the different skills involved. Skills there certainly are, and we shall look at some of these later, but our primary reference point for listening in this section is not so much skills and techniques as ministry – one that should be encouraged and practised in every church both amongst its own members and as a pastoral resource for the local community. The ears of the Body of Christ need to be alert and functioning if they are to be of any use.

In the New Testament, ministry is chiefly about service, of the kind demonstrated daily by Jesus. It is not about status and position but availability to serve, often in unspectacular ways yet always in the spirit of the Christ who stooped to wash feet. Listening is a footwashing ministry, in the first place to do with attitudes rather than skills – availability, compassion, belief in people – knowing from our own experience what being heard can do for us. Like any other ministry it will include times of perplexity, frustration, tiredness, disappointment, but there will also be times of joy, excitement, wonder and thanksgiving as we see what the apparent simplicity of being listened to can do for others.

Three images that, for me, describe the ministry of listening are gift, hospitality and healing. Being listened to, whether for five or fifty minutes, can feel a great gift, being listened to *and* heard an even greater one. At a hospice conference on bereavement, an older clergyman shared with a partner an experience of personal loss. His partner simply listened with full attention. Afterwards the clergyman spoke of the 'absolute luxury' of being listened to – for ten whole minutes! It was a small enough offering yet the gift received had been one of acceptance and worth, being valued and taken seriously as someone worth listening to. When listened to and heard in this way, we know that we matter – not only to the other person but to God whose availability is fleshed out in the listener. Moreover this gift often turns out to be mutual rather than one-way, for the listener, in giving, also receives – the trust, confidence and vulnerability of the one who turns to him.

As well as gift, listening is also about hospitality, the offering to someone of space in which to feel welcomed, met and safe, free to be himself, to be listened to and heard. Henri Nouwen calls listening 'the highest form of hospitality', of the sort that does not set out 'to change people but to offer them space where change can take place . . . hospitality is not a subtle invitation to adopt the lifestyle of the host, but the gift of a chance for the guest to find his own'.[1]

It is so easy to pile in with good advice before it is asked for, solutions which the listener may have found helpful but which may not fit the speaker. We need a servant spirit of humility to offer, in the first place, our personal space rather than our words, yet a space where we are fully present and available to the one needing our listening. Interestingly, in the Bible hospitality is not optional but obligatory. Yet, just as in listening the gift turns out to be mutual not one-sided, so in offering hospitality the host also receives, often surprisingly, from his visitor. When Elijah went to the widow at Zarephath for food and shelter, she was given by her visitor not only oil and meal but also the restoration to life of her dead son (1 Kings 17:9–24). I have so often found in listening that I am given far more than I offered and there is a mutuality of exchange and gratitude. True, the hospitality of listening can be costly for if the space offered is to be genuine then I as listener need to put aside my own preoccupations and concerns in order to be fully present and available to the other person. We cannot put on a show of hospitality, for any sensitive person will soon pick this up and back off in case he is a nuisance.

John Powell writes:

> I cannot merely appear to be interested in you and what you
> are saying while I am in fact distracted by many other things.
> I must experience and convey the reality to you that my
> time, my mind and my heart are yours, and that there is no
> one more important to me in the whole world right now than
> you.[2]

So this kind of listening demands sincerity. It is more to do
with quality than quantity and can be experienced in a chance
meeting or during a telephone call. It is chiefly about being
fully present to the other person and open to God on his or
her behalf. When Paul Tournier, the Swiss doctor, was in
general practice, he thought he knew all about his patients until
suddenly they began to talk to him on a deeper level. He said,
'The level on which our patients are prepared to talk to us
depends on the level of our own availability'.[3] This willingness
to put aside our own concerns is costly yet, freely given, it can
feel to the person needing a listening ear like stepping from a
cold, dark street into a warm, welcoming home.

As well as gift and hospitality, listening is also healing. I
shall never forget the time of my Confirmation when I hit a
very low patch. As a college lecturer with a strong professional
front it seemed to me important to soldier on alone, defences
held high. But behind the mask I felt isolated, frightened and
despairing. I also felt ashamed to feel like that, especially when
I was being joyfully received into the arms of mother Church!
I was a private person who found it hard to trust enough to
share the blackness and fear which I didn't want to own. The
Confirmation service was a good one but I felt numb before,
during and after it. Only later did I start to discover in a new
and amazing way what membership of the Church really meant
when Cynthia, my vicar's wife, and John, the curate, found the
time to listen to me at length. It was in the loving, hospitable
space they gave me that Christ came to bring healing to painful
places of inner hurt. I felt I had never before in my life been
listened to like that – which was, in itself, healing. As they

offered compassion and discernment, so I was able to start opening up the pain of years.

Nouwen wrote, 'Healing means, first of all, the creation of an empty but friendly space where those who suffer can tell their story to someone who can listen with real attention'.[4] I certainly found that in that friendly space I began not only to trust two people who were there for me but also the Christ they incarnated. If this was reception into the Church then it began to make sense after all. As I look back to that time, I still think and feel about it as a time of gift, hospitality and healing, the sort of ministry Jesus was constantly offering to those he met.

2

Qualities in the Listener

Dame Cicely Saunders, founder of the Hospice movement in this country, said, 'When someone is in a climate of listening he'll say things he wouldn't have said before'. What makes for this 'climate of listening' so that people are enabled to speak freely and know they are not alone on their journey?

Robert Carkhuff, an American psychologist, analysed many counselling interviews and their outcome in terms of personal change and extracted six dimensions or attributes that made for effectiveness. He also pointed out something rather startling – that good listening is not the preserve of the professionals. Ordinary lay people can prove equally effective as they offer what, in fact, turns out to be a therapeutic relationship.[5] Obviously this does not put the professionals out of a job, but it does mean there is plenty of scope for lay people to listen in such a way that people will grow and move forward. Michael Jacobs suggests that 'there is a mystique which is all too prevalent in our society, that it is only the expert who can carry out certain functions . . . we have as a society effectively deskilled the ordinary man or woman in those tasks which are part of common life'.[6] So long as lay people can recognise their limitations, be open to supervision and know when someone needs professional help, they can prove extremely effective as listeners.

Although this is not a textbook on listening, it is worth outlining these six dimensions as part of a good listener's offering and skill.[7] **Respect** is about giving value to the other person, affirming him as unique, worthwhile, made in God's image whether he acknowledges it or not. It is that attitude which says 'you are free to be yourself without risk of blame'. This is not the same as blandly accepting and condoning his sins or hurts. When the Pharisees dragged an adulteress to Jesus, he showed her great respect and also told her not to sin again. Respect includes not only seeing the person as she is now but seeing too what she is in process of becoming. It is not respectful to label people as 'problems', even when they see themselves that way. Paul wrote, 'Honour one another above yourselves' (Romans 12:10) or 'be eager to show respect for one another' (TEV). Gilbert Chesterton wrote of St Francis,

> He honoured all men; that is, he not only loved but respected them all . . . from the Pope to the beggar, from the Sultan of Syria . . . to the ragged robbers crawling out of the wood, there was never a man who looked into those brown burning eyes without being certain that Francis was really interested in *him*, in his own inner individual life from the cradle to the grave.[8]

Respecting also means resisting the temptation of looking for carbon copies of ourselves in others or classifying them as certain 'types'. So this will mean 'resisting our desire for order and coherence, and allowing the strangeness and newness of *this* person's experience to clutter up our attention'.[9] I like his 'clutter up' for it reminds me how I am in a relationship of mutuality rather than control.

Genuineness, a second dimension, is about being real and open rather than playing a role. A person needing to be heard deserves our reality rather than a façade. If I am being genuine I am seeking a consistency of word and action, not playing phoney or insincere. I may be listening to you but I also am on my own journey towards wholeness and this should characterise me, whether I talk about it or not. There will be times when sharing my own experiences is helpful, other times when I withhold my experiences but not myself from you. There can be something subtly deceptive about the person who nods and smiles appearing to be present, yet whose attention is really elsewhere. It is easy to play-act at listening especially if our own friendships are thin and we can, quite unconsciously, start feeding off our own listening role.

Respect and genuineness are part of **empathy** – another important quality in the listener. It means not 'to feel like' (that is sympathy) but 'to feel with'. It is about seeing the world through the other person's eyes, being accurately aware of her feelings and attempting to put them into words. Michael Jacobs suggests two steps in exercising empathy. The first is to register my own feelings and thoughts about what the speaker is saying. If Brian says that his mother died suddenly after he had argued with her, I might first ask myself the question, how would *I* feel? Probably guilty. At the same time I'll need to remember that his reactions may differ from mine, though the question may provide clues. The second and most important step is to leave my own feelings aside and enter into Brian's, asking myself, 'What is *he* feeling in the situation?' So I try a tentative question: 'I wonder if you're feeling guilty about that?' He may continue, 'Yes, very – but also angry and I can't understand that.' I respond, 'So as well as feeling guilty, you're also feeling angry' – my empathetic response means Brian knows he is being heard and understood, so he can continue and go deeper.

A fourth dimension is **concreteness**, or helping a person to avoid vagueness and be specific. It is easy for some people to hide in generalisations and thereby avoid the concrete, specific and personally relevant details. Sally, a bright young graduate with a good mind but underdeveloped in the area of her feelings, needed to learn how to share events, situations and relationships specifically so that she could begin to discover a vocabulary of feelings, shades and nuances in her everyday life. I might ask:

'How have you been feeling lately?'
'I don't know – perhaps a bit low.'
'Would you like to share some of the things that have been happening to you since we last met?'

In this way she learnt to share herself more specifically. Towards the end of our time together I might ask: 'Is there anything particular that has struck you in what we've been sharing?'

Sometimes we would clarify specific actions she could take based on what we had been sharing – a phone call, a letter, talking to one of her parents. Gradually she began to move from experiencing her world as monochrome to experiencing it as many-coloured.

A fifth dimension is **confrontation**, though rarely appropriate in the early stages of listening. The word can sound aggressive as though the listener has suddenly turned judge. Michael Jacobs writes, 'Confrontation is not a means of trying to catch a person out, of making him appear small, or of punishing him . . . neither is it the iron fist in the velvet glove, but rather the "still small voice" which speaks more clearly than the earthquake, wind and fire.'[10] He also points out that it should not be used if a listener is feeling angry towards the other person or if there is, as yet, insufficient rapport between them. But appropriately used, confrontation is a great gift, part of the respect and care which can enable a person to become aware of discrepancies, and take responsibility for change and growth. It is when we know what is going on that we can do something about it, yet sometimes even our best friends won't tell us!

I think of Christine, a gifted but anxious perfectionist who could quickly paralyse herself into all sorts of imagined inabilities by constantly comparing herself with others and always coming off the worse. A friend, noting how often this happened and the depressing consequences, asked her, 'Would it be helpful for you to look at the way you compare yourself so much with others and what that is doing to you?' The effect on Christine, far from plunging her into depression, was like a light being switched on. Obviously the relationship has to be safe otherwise the person may become defensive, distancing or attacking. Always the underlying motive should be one of caring enough to want the best for the other person. And, to discover our best, we need each other. Carkhuff points out how confrontation draws attention to the responsibility for adopting adult responses to real-life situations and for risking new integrations of behaviour. And if, on the receiving end, we feel rather chilly and exposed, still the gift being offered us is for our personal growth.

Carkhuff's sixth dimension is **immediacy** – that awareness of what is going on here and now between listener and speaker and the ability to share it openly. How is the speaker experiencing me as a listener? How do I as listener experience the speaker? This may not be shared explicitly in the early stages of listening before the relationship is established, but can be a very helpful resource later on. If someone has been sharing personally, he may be left feeling very vulnerable. As a listener I might ask:

'How are you feeling with me at the moment?'
'Rather silly and thinking I must be wasting your time.'
'So you are feeling rather silly. I was thinking it takes courage to talk like that. I certainly don't feel you're wasting my time.'

It is far better that fears and fantasies are checked out rather than left lurking uncomfortably in the shadows. As listener I should also be aware of my own feelings and reactions as I listen. 'What is happening in the relationship now that I feel bored? or anxious? or wanting to fall asleep?' 'What is happening as we seem to be going round in circles?' 'How am I feeling towards this person now?' Perhaps I am feeling impatient, unsure if he is making any progress, wishing he would stop telling stories about his past and stay with his present questions. It might be helpful to share this insight (though not necessarily the impatience) with the speaker, inviting him to find a way of looking at the present. When the connection between what I am feeling and what is being shared is not immediately obvious, I might usefully talk this over with a supervisor so that I can continue to grow in self-understanding. It is as we own, clarify and take responsibility for what is going on within that we shall learn to walk in the light rather than live in the ambiguities and distortions of shadowland.

These six dimensions are partly a channelling and focussing

of what we already are (or are in process of becoming), and partly skills to be learnt and refined. But having them does not necessarily depend on any particular belief system. What difference, if any, will it make to be a Christian listener?

Alastair Campbell looks helpfully at the Christian quality of integrity in the carer. He maintains that 'all genuine care for those assailed by doubt and guilt proceeds from this integrity and without it no ecclesiastical role or counselling technique will be of help to others'.[11] He sees integrity as 'steadfastness', an inner strength, wisdom, wholeness, tested and refined by life's experiences, personal yet somehow embracing more than myself. Integrity is harder to define than to recognise and we are often drawn to that sort of person long before we try to analyse what it is in them that we need for our own growth.

Looking back, we may well recall individuals like this who have meant something to us at particular, sometimes crucial, points on our life journey. For me, it was Sylvia Lake, wife of the well-known Dr Frank, yet with an experience and contribution very much her own. I first met her when training as a Clinical Theology tutor. She certainly displayed Carkhuff's six dimensions but it went beyond that – there was an honesty, humanity, wisdom and wholeness about her which were, for many of us, a 'fleshing out' of integrity. She was 'fully human, fully alive', in touch with both joy and pain. And, as I discovered in the times when she listened to me, there was a quality of loving in her that was resilient, straight and unsentimental. Gordon Allport, the Harvard psychologist, said that love as described in 1 John 4 is 'incomparably the greatest psychotherapeutic agent – something that professional psychiatry cannot of itself create, focus nor release'.[12] This was so with Sylvia. Certainly it was more than a collection of human qualities that attracted me, rather a uniting of them into what felt both personal and beyond personality. She was at home in her humanity yet at the same time pointing beyond herself. At various points when I have been depressed I have turned to Sylvia and been helped, not only by her good listening skills but by something deeper – the presence of grace and God in her. I can think of others who, in similar ways, have been given to me at various, often critical, points in my life. They may or may not have been trained in counselling skills, which has helped me to see that, 'In the last analysis there is no cleverness or accomplishment in pastoral care. It is no more (and no less) than sharing with another in the experience of grace, a surprising, unsought gift.'[13]

Ultimately, however skilled we may be, it is this grace, Christ at the centre, which really matters. Not that this undercuts the need for training but it is a reminder that finding our centre in God and being constantly drawn back to him, as surely as a compass needle is to its north pole, is what really counts. The prayerful life is not one in which we say frequent prayers but one in which nothing is done, said or listened to independently of God, so that all we are is permeated by him.

'The essence is to be established in the remembrance of God and to walk in his presence.'[14] This 'being established' has become, for me, the priority in pastoral care. And it was only in time that I discovered the hidden and costly ministry of prayer that is central in Sylvia's life.

Good listeners will find they are in demand and the temptation, at least for some, will be to become more and more available. But Nouwen writes, 'the Bible does not seem to support this. Jesus' primary concern was to be obedient to his Father, to live constantly in his presence. Only then did it become clear to him what his task was in relationships with people'.[15]

Above all, the Christian listener is to be a 'living reminder' of God and one whose whole life incarnates the gifts and graces of Christ.

What are we Listening to?

A Dutch *Rule for a new brother* reads,

> Obedience also demands of you
> that you listen to the other person;
> not only to what he is saying
> but to what he is.
> Then you will begin to live in such a way
> that you neither crush nor dominate
> nor entangle your brother
> but help him to be himself
> and lead him to freedom.[16]

What does it mean to listen like this? It is one thing to follow what a person is saying but we also need to understand what he means by the particular words he uses and the way he says them. How do I know what David means when our dialogue goes like this:

Me: How are you, David?
David: Grim –
Me: What's been happening then?
David: I've had a grim week –

Is he ill? Has he had a row with his wife? Has work been difficult? I'll need to find out what 'grim' means for him. Also, what is happening *in* him when he talks faster and faster so that I get increasingly tense? Or what is happening in Joan as her voice sounds so monotonous I start nodding off? A person's manner of speaking is saying something that I need to hear, not as a detached, clinical observer or critic but so that I experience her as she really is. Too often we select what we will see and know in others. Our relationships are rarely unaffected by our own projections. Knowing a person for what he or she is calls for a patient, profound listening that most of us are unused to.

We must listen too with our eyes for, before ever a person opens her mouth to speak, she is communicating messages about herself. 'Body language' is an important and complex means of communication. Watch how two people enter a house in completely different ways. Laura comes through the front door with her head down, apart from a quick anxious glimpse at me, her inert body creeping rather than walking up the stairs and she doesn't utter a word. Gina enters head up, open-faced with a warm smile, stretching out both arms in greeting and chattering all the way up the stairs. Our bodies often describe our spirits – the slumped or upright shoulders, the hands that are relaxed or that pluck nervously at a sleeve, the body that flings itself in abandonment into a chair or sits tensely on the edge. But, again, to listen with our eyes is not so that we can reach a cool, clinical appraisal of the other but that we might receive her as she is in her entirety. Alastair Campbell writes, 'the looking which enhances such encounter comes from the desire to know, not to know *about*, the other person'.[17] It has been said that 'the eyes are the gateway to the soul'. Some people feel free to share their soul, others don't. I think of Brian, a theological student with considerable pain and hurt in his past. It took many months of regular meetings before he could begin to look up from the carpet into my face. I received it as a great gift the day it happened. We need sensitivity to know what eye contact a person wants (and doesn't want) from us. For some it is nurturing but for others frightening. If we are there to offer rather than to demand, then we shall need to learn flexibility in the ways we look at them.

We must also listen to a person's feelings. Some are free in expressing a whole spectrum of feelings – joy, delight, excitement, fear, annoyance, fury – others are not and maybe are frightened of emotions, their own and other people's, so keep them hidden. Our upbringing, our cultural and religious background affect us all – one person may have grown up in a family where there was great freedom to express emotions, another in a family where certain feelings were acceptable (e.g. love, affection, happiness) but others not so (e.g. anger, fear, sexual feelings). Emotions are, of themselves, neither 'right' nor 'wrong', it is what we do with them that matters. A good listener will need to have made friends with the colourful spectrum of his own emotions if he is to become open and available to those of others. And if we, or those we listen to, are scared at what we find, it is by facing the truth of our own humanity rather than repressing it that we discover what we can do about it. Elizabeth Kubler-Ross said that until we discover the Hitler in us we cannot discover the St Teresa.

This kind of listening will involve a faithful hearing of the feelings people express and also a deeper listening beneath what we can hear with our ears and see with our eyes. Michael Jacobs calls it hearing 'the bass line'. He writes, 'This aspect of listening is like trying to spot the bass line of a piece of music, while still concentrating upon the melody on the top line'.[18] It is about attending to and drawing out a person's deeper feelings which he may, as yet, be only partly conscious of himself. Underneath Michael's adult and articulate use of words and upright bearing was a frightened eight-year-old, feeling abandoned at boarding school and having to learn to fight to keep up with the others. It was because someone listened to him with respect and sensitivity that a part of himself he had with good reason hidden away, was now able to surface, be re-experienced, respected, owned, wept over, shared, and thus become part of his ministry to others. God does not 'send' painful experiences to children but he can undoubtedly rework them into the fabric of a person's life so that he and others are enriched. This is the paradox at the heart of the 'wounded healer' and it comes not through the denial or suppression of pain but through acknowledging and owning it.

This deeper listening to others is costly. Harry Williams wrote, 'it is perhaps the hardest work in which we ever engage, but it results in our discovery of their loveableness, hidden though it may sometimes be under successive layers of repellent distortion'.[19] This struck me forcibly in listening to an eighty-year-old widower, Fred, reclusive in life-style, his hands, feet and head covered with the sores and scabs of psoriasis. Whenever he spoke he was full of the woes of life. Yet one day as I tuned into the 'bass line' of his fear of death, his vulnerability and loveableness became far more important than his bleeding sores. Somehow Fred's outer sores and scars reminded me of my inner ones. It was not so much a Good Samaritan relationship as one of mutuality. I wept when he died. There were only three people at his funeral. Fred had given me much for 'the more a person realises the fact of his co-inherence in others, the more he becomes his own true self'.[20]

We must also listen to a person's thinking. Paul wrote, 'let God transform you inwardly by a complete change of your mind' (Romans 12:2 TEV). Such transformation is the work of a lifetime, for most of us live with much untruth about ourselves, others, the world we live in and God. We need to listen to what people are thinking about themselves, their 'theme songs' which are, often unconsciously to them, being sung out loud and clear to others – 'nothing ever goes right for me', 'I'm God's gift to humanity', 'I'm no good', etc. To be in a relationship where a person can hear, through his listener, his theme song, is asking for considerable trust, yet it is only as we know, that we can begin to change.

Our thinking about God may also be distorted and in need of revision. 'When the half gods go, the real God comes' (C. S. Lewis) and sometimes the God we cherish in our head is quite different from the one in our heart. Rationally I may believe that God is love yet in my heart fear his punishment. Once at a conference, in the discussion group following a lecture, we were looking at the question, 'What kind of God do I believe in?' A very gifted and respected Christian surgeon, who is also a non-stipendiary minister, began some lively discussion when he said, 'When I am not operating and not preaching, I feel guilty'. As we discussed, most of us realised we also, to a lesser or greater extent, shared his belief in a slave-driver God.

Amongst the words a person uses, his body language, his feeling and thinking, we need also to listen to his silences which can mean many things. There is the reflective, thoughtful silence when he is considering something that has been said, or working something out. There is the shocked silence when a person is stunned and there seem no words for what has happened. There is the stubborn silence, often reflected by the set of the mouth or jaw which says, 'I'm not going to say a word, so there!' There is the embarrassed silence often reflected in a person's body language too. And there is the peaceful silence perhaps following a moment of shared joy, wonder or contentment, when words would distract.

The listener must learn not simply to tolerate silences but to listen to them and discern when to ask, 'Would you like to share what you're thinking?' *and* when not to. And she must herself become comfortable with silence. 'Silence has the power to force you to dig deep inside yourself.'[21] The digging may be painful but often it is in staying with the silence rather than escaping into words that we discover (to our surprise) the buried treasure within.

Listening to someone then is a multi-dimensional activity, complex, demanding and mutually enriching for it is as we listen like this that we hear not only what someone is saying but also who he is.

4

Some Cautions

> I have just hung up; why did he telephone?
> I don't know . . . Oh, I get it . . .
> I talked a lot and listened very little.
>> Forgive me Lord,
>> It was a monologue and not a dialogue.[22]

At least the intending listener knew where she had gone wrong! It is all too easy to make mistakes in listening yet not realise it. Talking too much is just one example of how the desire to be helpful can sometimes manifest itself in unhelpful ways. For example, someone wants to unburden himself or clarify his understanding and we feel we must *say* something, give advice, solve his problem, comfort him, tell him our own story. Bonhoeffer wrote, 'Christians, especially ministers, so often think they must always contribute something when they are in the company of others, that this is the one service they have to render. They forget that listening can be a greater service than speaking'.[23]

Obviously there is a place for contributing something, but it can all too easily be done to meet the needs of the listener rather than the speaker. Advice-giving, for example, clearly has its place but can also lead to an over-dependence on the listener which can prevent a person from growing up. Some people, whose very need is to learn responsibility in making their own decisions, are only too happy to be spoon-fed with advice or suggestions. Unchecked, this can develop into a collusive relationship, each gratifying the needs of the other. Similarly a listener may, in his anxiety to help, press for premature solutions before he has heard the person through or the heart of the matter has been reached. I watched a skilled listener working with Betty who had asked for help but couldn't seem to describe the need. The listener did not rush in to suggest, interpret or comfort. After half an hour the listener suggested in a warm, friendly way that Betty went home *with* her frustration and that, at the right time, she would discover what she really wanted to share. Which is exactly what happened – the frustration served a purpose and Betty found a way forward. In Jesus' ministry of healing he often asked people, 'What do you want me to do for you?' Presumably he knew the need yet for the person to discover and put into words what he wanted was an integral part of the healing. Listening in such a way that we facilitate the person to do his or her own work is to give maximum opportunity for growth.

A listener must also resist the temptation to take over by telling her own story, reminiscing or wandering down memory lane. There is a right time for sharing oneself and one's experiences, but the wisdom and ways forward I have found will not always be what you need. On one occasion this happened to me and I emerged feeling angry and cheated after the so-called listener did all the talking, resulting in a messy role reversal! We are strangely resistant to the belief that often what is needed more than words, advice or stories is the simple presence of someone who can listen and care.

There are other areas too where the listener will need self-discipline, such as restraining one's personal reactions to what is being said. Some of the things people will share will be hard to listen to, involving, as they may, cruelty, pain, injustice. It is all too easy to respond by expressing shock, panic, anger or blame. It is not that the listener is to be unfeeling or passive in the face of pain but rather that one is there for the *other* person rather than oneself, offering a safe and personal space for him to share what he wants. It is also inappropriate and confusing (though all too easy) to bring in one's own feelings from another situation or relationship. If, for example, I am angry at something that happened earlier today and have not yet dealt with my feelings, I might direct them towards the speaker who may then feel blamed or punished. Or I might project my feelings on to him, seeing him as the angry one rather than myself. Later we shall look at the question of what the listener does with his own affairs in order to be fully available and uncluttered.

Another way we can be unhelpful is in our use of questions. There is an art and skill in asking questions that enable rather than divert a person. To be on the receiving end of a string of questions can feel like being under interrogation, e.g. 'So what did you tell your wife?', 'Then what did she say?', 'How did you react?', 'Why was that?' It can be very distracting for a person to be constantly interrupted by questions as he is telling his story or thinking aloud. Moreover, a listener needs to know *why* he is asking such questions – is it because he is anxious for more details or to enable the speaker to move forward? 'Why' questions are generally unhelpful, encouraging a person into offering intellectual explanations and leaving feelings unexplored. Ask questions sparingly and in order to help a person be more specific or to open up an area. 'How' questions generally do this, e.g. 'How are you feeling in that difficult relationship?' rather than 'Why are you having difficulty in that relationship?'

A useful distinction is between 'closed' and 'open' questions. 'Closed' questions lead to a closed response – a 'yes' or 'no' answer, e.g. 'Have you felt low this week?' They also suggest the sort of answer expected and the only way to follow up closed questions is to ask more. 'Open' questions invite an opening up of what the speaker is saying, generally begin with 'How?', 'What?', 'In what way?' and help a person explore and think aloud. A useful form of open question can be to take up a word or phrase used by the speaker and reflect it back, e.g.

Janet: I felt awful when he said that to me.
Listener: Can you say more about the awful feeling?

In this way, Janet has the chance to explore her feelings further and find out more about what is happening in her.[24] Often, as trust develops in a listening relationship and the speaker is more forthcoming, the need for questions will lessen.

Areas for caution abound in listening. The important thing is not to be too dismayed when we do not listen as well as we might, but to become aware of what happened, perhaps with the help of someone more experienced than we are, and go on learning.

5

The Process of Listening

Good listening is therapeutic. The story is told of a refugee psychiatrist who, on his arrival in America, needed work as soon as possible. With his exceedingly limited English he received his first patient. After an hour of attentive listening (with hardly a word spoken by the psychiatrist) the patient left, profuse in her thanks for the help she had received! – And certainly there are those times when 'just listening' meets the need, because what is chiefly required is not dialogue or advice but simple presence. I find it happens quite often on the phone. Eileen's husband, Tim, was dying of cancer at home. Although some relatives were staying with them, Eileen needed to pour out all the details – the operation, the treatment, the nursing, the pain, fear and anguish of it all. I said very little but was simply there for her, unseen but present. Similar outpourings sometimes happen after a church service or during a visit in the parish or even in the local supermarket. It is often at times when I least expect it that people need a listening ear. It was once said of Bishop Trevor Huddleston that, whether he was with someone for three minutes or three hours, that person had his full and undivided attention. At such times it is availability of spirit that we chiefly need, to give ourselves simply and attentively to the other, believing that not only are we a gift to them but so can they be to us.

At other times, however, the listener will be able to prepare himself. If someone has asked me for listening time I try to build in personal preparation, however short. I need to be open to God both for myself and for the person coming. I take note of my thoughts, feelings, distractions and consciously open them to God. Quite often the last thing I feel like doing is to listen to someone and it is helpful to acknowledge this and realise that my own resources *are* inadequate. Sometimes I uncurl my fingers and simply hold out empty hands to God. I seek to be still in God's presence and not to fear my own emptiness or distractedness or inadequacy. 'Provided only that you consent . . . the work of grace is going on in you through the whole business of living, to hollow you out, to make you capax Dei . . . able to receive God'.[25] And this receiving of God is important if we are to be available to him for the person. I also hold the person by name into the love and light of God, asking that what we need will be given.

The best meeting place is one where disturbances will be minimal – telephone, children, interruptions – and where we can sit in comfortable chairs at the same level. Dr Janet Goodall, a gifted paediatrician who sees her professional life in terms of ministry, makes a point of having her head lower than the child's or parent's when she is talking with them in the wards. The important thing is to communicate equality rather than superiority. The most comfortable positioning of the chairs is usually reckoned to be the 4 o'clock one so that eye contact is easy without being confronting. A box of tissues can save you from having to go in search. It can be helpful to fix a time limit beforehand, not only for your sake but also for the other person's, since it can help him to get into his subject rather than put it off. These practicalities simply make it easier to give full attention to the person needing a listening ear.

It is one thing to listen to someone who simply needs to pour out a torrent of words and feelings and then go away relieved, but what about the person who needs to find a way forward, clarify a muddle or reach a decision? What is the 'shape' of the listening time to be and how can the listener's responses help? There are many different approaches to this in the field of counselling and listening but some of the main ingredients are:

    i.   **building a relationship** between yourself and the other person

ii.   **exploring** what the person wants to share
iii. **understanding** together what is going on
iv.   **stimulating action** when appropriate
v.   **encouraging the person to apply** what he is learning

i. Building the relationship[26]

Setting a person at ease is an important first step in establishing a good relationship. The way we welcome her can communicate acceptance and warmth or can confirm her worst fears that she is being a nuisance and should not have come. To use her name is to acknowledge and affirm her personal identity; to offer a handshake if we don't know her well, can give that contact which helps her feel aware of support. Some people know exactly where they are going to begin, others are uncertain. So I might say, 'Take your time to decide where to begin'. If she does take time, resist the temptation to fill in the gaps – simply relax and wait. Once the words start coming, listen carefully, watch sensitively and don't be afraid of silences. Try to remember the details (e.g. the children's names, order of events, etc.) and avoid interrupting. The quality of our concern and interest will communicate as we are quietly there, with and for the other person. We need, especially at an early stage, to resist the temptation to ask too many questions.

ii. and iii. Exploring and understanding

At the heart of creative listening is the understanding that we are, in partnership, participating in a process. As John speaks out, his thinking and feelings will begin to surface and become conscious. One way in which John can hear himself is for his listener to use a process of reflective listening called 'mirroring', which can be very helpful for many, though not all, listening situations.[27] It takes time and practice to use well and is best learnt in a practical setting with supervision. I include it here not to teach it but to illustrate a way forward.

As the speaker proceeds, the listener reflects back what he is saying, summarising facts but reflecting back feeling words in full. So the listener may ask:

'John, may I check that I have heard you correctly?', then summarises the facts John has shared but includes all his feeling words.

Our most helpful contribution is to listen and reflect back rather than interrupt, interpret or advise. If John uses no feeling words it can be helpful to ask: 'How are you feeling about that?'

We may, from time to time, invite him to go deeper by asking the question, 'Would you like to say more about that?' When we sense that he has explored what he needs to, we should ask: 'John, what for you is at the heart of all you have been saying?'

We need to hear *his* perception at this stage for he will only move forward as he is ready to do so. It is often at this point that something important is clarified. As he responds, again it is helpful for the listener to reflect back his words so that he can hear what he is thinking.

iv. and v. Stimulating action and encouraging a person to apply what he is learning

Having helped John to explore, focus and understand what is going on – and this may take some time – it is important to consider what can be done about it. So the listener asks: 'Is there anything you need to do about this?'

It may take him time to clarify this but, again, the listener should reflect back what he says until John is clear where he is going from here and is encouraged forward.

In describing one particular approach I am not suggesting it is the only way to listen. We are not to be servants of methods or techniques but rather allow them to serve those we listen to. Disciplined listening is not about rigidity but about creating in us deeper availability to the one we are listening to and to God.

An example:
My elderly Aunt Cath, after several falls, was hurriedly admitted to a local authority old people's home. I was the family member nearest to where she was and felt anxious as to whether she should stay there or move to a more pleasant home. I asked Margaret to listen to me and we agreed that she should use the process of mirroring described. She asked, 'Where would you like to begin?'

I described Auntie Cath's situation while Margaret listened without interrupting then, in summary form, reflected back to me what I had said. I was feeling anxious, guilty that I couldn't have her to live with me, panicky about what could be done in the time available. Margaret reflected back these feeling words to me, 'So you're feeling anxious, guilty and panicky as to what you should be doing.' Sometimes she asked: 'Would you like to say more about that?' I elaborated and she asked: 'How do you feel about that?'

Gradually, and to my surprise, I found that I was feeling a great deal, including memories of my mother whom I had been with in her terminal illness two and a half years earlier. Suddenly I wept. Margaret quietly said it was all right to cry and waited. Then she asked: 'What do you feel is at the heart of what you've been saying, Anne?' I found myself replying: 'I want Auntie Cath to die knowing she is loved.' This came as a surprise since I'd started by thinking I wanted to clarify a practical matter. Margaret asked: 'Do you want to say more about that?' I was grateful to explore further for a few minutes. Then Margaret said, 'Is there anything you feel you need to do in the light of what you've been saying?'

Three points emerged – to ensure that the warden of the home was given a recently changed family phone number and that he knew where to contact our family in case of need; to look at some alternative homes; and to spend time more regu-

larly with Auntie Cath. Margaret reflected these back to me,
which felt helpful. Then she asked me if I would like us to
pray. I agreed and she prayed specifically that Auntie Cath
would die knowing she was loved. I suddenly felt a great burden
had been lifted.

In the following weeks I visited two pleasant homes for the
elderly but Auntie Cath made it quite clear to me that she
wanted to stay where she was. I visited her whenever possible.
Then suddenly, in the middle of a working week involving
much travel, on the one night I was at home the warden phoned
me to say he thought Auntie Cath was dying. I drove to her
late that night and was able to hold her in my arms as she died.
Amidst the sadness was a quiet sense of wonder that God had
used the listening time to clarify the heart of Auntie Cath's
need and what it was I wanted for her.

Reflective listening can be powerful and we should not use it
lightly for it can take a person deeper than was expected. Used
responsibly it can be creative and fruitful.

Some people may question the use of prayer in this way. In
the example described, it felt completely natural and appropriate for Margaret to ask if praying together seemed right, and
it did. But there should be nothing automatic about this. Some
will welcome spoken prayer, others will feel more comfortable
to sit silently in the presence of God, offering him what has
been shared, people who have been named, any decisions made
and any action to be taken. It can sometimes be important, as
we are quiet before God, for the listener to say, 'Let's listen
for anything God might be saying'. The listener or speaker may
want to share an insight, a Bible verse or a picture that has
come to mind in the silence. It is important to allow time for
this for the Holy Spirit may be at work in the person in ways
beyond our own.

Recently, after listening to Tom's painful story, we were
silent for a time then I felt prompted to say, 'Tom, I believe
that God is wanting to say that he is *for* you.' Tom received
this gratefully with tears in his eyes and later wrote, 'Thank

you for the affirming as well as the realism – I needed that more than I thought'. Sometimes it will not be appropriate to suggest prayer with the person, but it can still be an important part of the background ministry to the person with whom the listener is involved.

6

Sensitive Areas

Listening inevitably involves us in moving into sensitive areas where we are constantly faced with the complexities of human nature. 'Just listening' can often leave us feeling we shall be wearing our 'L' plates into eternity!

i. Confidentiality

It can feel shattering to share a confidence and then discover it has been leaked out. A listener must honour what is shared with him so that the speaker knows he is trustworthy. Discretion and self-discipline will be needed and sometimes we shall feel lonely as we are left holding people's secrets. What can we do with them? I can sometimes experience a physical sense of relief in offering back to God what has been heard, thought about, felt and pictured, especially when the details are vivid and painful. And this offering is not simply for the listener's sake but is a way of bringing that person to the God who is constantly active in re-working the fabric of our lives.

Sometimes a person will begin by anxiously saying, 'You won't tell anyone about this, will you . . . ?' It is easy to fall into the trap of agreeing before one has a clue of the content. Perhaps information will be needed beyond what we ourselves can supply (e.g. legal or financial) and without which the person's progress may be hindered. If so, it is best to ask for his permission and to give reasons for this. It may even be helpful to consult the third party together.

But as well as the speaker sometimes needing help from a

third party, so does the listener who will, from time to time, need to look at what is happening for him in the listening relationship. A good listener who wants to go on learning will need a 'senior partner', someone with more experience in listening than himself, perhaps someone with supervision skills whose concern is to help the listener to see more clearly what is happening in the relationship and to work through any blocks or difficulties that arise. In this sense a listener must always retain the right to consult.

But is it ever right to break confidence in other ways? Very occasionally, yes. If, for example, a wife confided in you that her husband was abusing their child, it would be irresponsible to keep confidence and delay the possibility of getting further help. But hopefully this would be a rare exception.

ii. Boundaries

Another sensitive area is that of observing boundaries – and I am thinking particularly here of the listener's recognition of her own boundaries of competence. It can quickly happen that, as I listen to someone, I begin to realise that the problem is far more complex than I had thought and I am soon feeling out of my depth. A person may say something that sounds off an alarm bell within us. On one occasion Karen, a married woman, in her forties, asked for my help. She described the difficulty she had in feeling or expressing her emotions and the consequent strain in her marriage. As I listened it seemed to me there were various possible ways forward. But suddenly she seemed to change gear and, with an expressionless face, told me of fiercely destructive moods which could suddenly rise up within, making her want to jump through a window or destroy someone. An alarm bell sounded within me and I found myself wishing she could see a certain psychiatrist. I told Karen I thought we needed help beyond what I could offer and, although somewhat taken aback, she was open to this. Amazingly, the catchment area Karen lived in was served by the psychiatrist in question. An appointment was made and my role changed from listening to praying. She and her partner are moving forward into healing and growth.

A listener is one link in a chain, part of a network of different helps available. It is not failure to know when our own level of competence has been reached or when we suddenly feel out of depth. Indeed, a good listener will learn to ask herself questions to check this out:

— As far as I can see, is A. moving forward as I listen to her? Or is she stuck? Or are we going round in circles?
— Are there other resources that could help A. at present?
— What are my feelings as I listen to A. and do they tell me anything? (e.g. am I feeling bored? Dreading our next meeting? Angry?)
— Is A. meeting certain needs in me as I listen to her? (e.g. my need to be needed.) How is this affecting the relationship?

A listener needs to know when she is helping *and* when she is not and this again is where a 'senior partner' can be very useful. Joyce Huggett writes:

I can be content to be just one spoke in the wheel of a person's life. I need never masquerade as the Messiah. Omni-competent. I need not even make apology for my limitations. On the contrary, I can feel comfortable working within them; content to leave other parts of the burden to those with different expertise.[28]

Hopefully, as listeners function within the church or community, there can come a growing awareness of other resource people so that a local network of support and care can develop that will include both lay and professional people, each recognising the contribution of the others.

iii. Dependency

When listening is going well a person can easily become over-dependent on the listener. This is acceptable as a stage of growth but is certainly not the goal. Maturity in relationships is not about dependence or independence but rather our inter-dependence which recognises that each of us has strengths *and* weaknesses, each of us is to give to *and* receive from others. A hurting person will not ultimately be helped by leaning more and more heavily upon me, though my support and encourage-ment may well be part of his healing. The listener should be careful not to invite or prolong dependence on himself. Of course it can be flattering to know I am needed and am part of someone else's growth and healing. Yet this can, often quite unconsciously, meet my own need for significance. The greater sense of satisfaction should come as we see someone walking away from us grateful for what he has received and ready to face fresh challenges. Generally it is advisable that a man listens to a man and a woman to a woman. If this is not possible then the man listener might ask that a woman be present, quietly supporting and praying.

It was a wise listener who, having spent many hours listening to Derek, had a letter from him which read, 'Thank you for all your help and thank you that I no longer need you'. If we are attending to our own resources, we shall not be depending on those we help to be our means of resource, even though we shall be glad to have helped them.

iv. Defences[29]

We cannot listen to people for long before becoming aware of some of their defences and this is another sensitive area. When someone feels unable to own or share parts of himself (usually involving hurt), he puts up a defence or mask, generally quite unconsciously. Jenny may have formed the habit of crying rather than risking assertion. Brian may explode rather than expose his hurt or fear. Barbara may avoid her mother by being over-busy, not realising her own avoidance pattern. It is not part of the listener's work to rip off the masks, however clearly he can see what is behind them. Some defences we may need for our survival. But others we may in time choose to lower or remove, often because we sense there is a better way of living and relating. Perhaps we want to risk more vulnerability or we may see in someone else that integrity which, deep down, we ourselves seek. The listener's part is not to expose or judge but to invite openness by modelling it in himself.

In his pastoral encounters with individuals, Jesus did not tear down their defences though he was fully aware of the sins and shortcomings that lay behind them. He challenged Zacchaeus without putting him down (Luke 19), corrected Nicodemus without disrespecting him (John 3), confronted the Samaritan woman without destroying her (John 4). It was only the Pharisees and Sadducees he attacked for their mask-wearing. They were the 'hypocrites' (literally 'play actors') deliberately pretending to be who they were not and flaunting their supposed strengths as religious virtues.

The listener, then, needs to exercise discernment in this area, inviting rather than demanding openness. To focus on someone's defences can cause him to defend and protect himself all the more and so make matters worse rather than better. The listener can best help by modelling what it is to be a person who is 'travelling' rather than 'arrived', by building a bridge of trust for the other to step on, by listening to God on his behalf, by being prepared to wait, by learning how to confront appropriately and supportively. In this way he may be given the great gift of seeing a person begin to lower his defences and move out into greater freedom.

7

Resources for Listening

Listening, like any worthwhile ministry, is tiring. It calls for concentration, commitment, faith, a putting aside of one's own preoccupations. As we listen in depth to another person we can be left feeling weary, depleted, sometimes anxious. How can we give ourselves generously yet remain resourced?

I once saw a lake in California sparkling like a little blue jewel in the sun. The bright reflected image of trees, rocks and sky was as clear as a mirror. The lake had an outlet where its water flowed out and an inlet where fresh water entered. With no outlet the water would become dirty, stagnant and congested with flotsam. With no inlet there would be no fresh supply of water. It was the two-way movement of the water that ensured its freshness. As we listen in a concentrated way to another person we are both affected by what we hear and we are giving out energy – energy which then needs to be replaced by a fresh infilling so that we are renewed and refreshed again.

Becoming resourced begins with knowing ourselves and what we need. Sometimes, for example, we shall need people, at other times space. As well as our many acquaintances we all need some quality relationships where we know ourselves to be fully accepted for who we are – warts and all. I could certainly not survive without that small inner circle of trusted friends who are committed to me even when I am at my most difficult. If I needed to, I could phone them in the middle of the night, howling and raving, and know that they still love me!

'When a man does not acknowledge to himself who, what, and how he is, he is out of touch with reality, and he will sicken . . . And . . . no man can come to know himself except as an outcome of disclosing himself to another person.'[30]

It is within such honest and growing relationships that we come to know ourselves and discover (to our relief) that we are not alone, that we too will be listened to and heard. Yet it can be all too easy to substitute the intimacy we should experience with those in our closest circle, by the intimacy experienced as listeners when we are, often temporarily, admitted to some of the personal details of someone else's life. Eugene Kennedy writes of this danger for counsellors and it applies equally to listeners:

> Helpers may ask – Is my emotional life fed in counselling? Do I get enough response there so that I limit . . . my emotional reactions in the other relationships in my life? . . . some counsellors lead most of their emotional lives in their offices and there is little left over when they return to their families – they are midway, in other words, between two intimate worlds, never entering either one of them fully and caught somewhere outside both camps . . . It is possible for the emotional commitment of therapy to draw away the kind of emotional commitment that should be present in marriage or in other relationships.[31]

If we are giving out to those we listen to at the expense of our growth in relationship, then there is something wrong. And using phrases like 'heavy demands', 'Christian availability', 'sacrificial ministry' is no excuse for not making time to foster the quality of relationship that each of us needs on our journey to maturity. We must make time to tend and refuel our closest relationships if they are to re-energise us as they should.

We shall also need, as suggested earlier, a wise senior partner or supervisor who will help us look at what we meet in the listening relationship in such a way that we can become more effective. I often find that as I speak out what feels like a muddled confusion, there will come – perhaps through a question or observation put to me – a clarifying of issues and movement forward again. This might happen in a one-to-one relationship or in a group. I belong to a supervision group that includes doctors, clergy, counsellors and teachers. We meet bi-monthly, listen to each other's pastoral work, especially any difficulties we are encountering, help each other find ways forward and pray for each other. In this way, we help to resource each other. Anyone involved in a lot of listening yet with no such support should discover if a social worker or counsellor could occasionally help by giving time for super-vision.

We should also be discovering what we need for our resourc-ing in the midst of daily life. Book titles like *Staying Sane under Stress*, *Ordering your Private World*, and *Ministry Burnout*,[32] indicate what often happens in pastoral work. The giving out that is involved needs deliberately to be countered by a taking in. For one person this may be through music-making, for others photography or reading, sport, bird-watching, wood-work. Sometimes, in the middle of a busy day, I discover a renewed sense of inner space and solitude by a leisurely walk around the garden. I deliberately slow down to look closely at the snowdrops amongst the ivy, the new green buds appearing on the trees, the clump of early tawny gold primulas, the cheerful robin, the smell of freshness and the blue and white streaked sky. I watch the Canada geese flying in formation with outstretched necks towards the gravel-pit ponds and spend a few moments talking to the donkey next door. Such times can help me become centred again, especially if I feel fragmented.

Physical exercise is also important as part of our resourcing, especially when listening means we are sitting still. Exercise can re-energise the whole of us, body, mind and spirit. In sedentary work our breathing can become shallow without our realising it, whereas exercise makes us breathe more deeply and revitalises us at every level. Swimming does this for me and what can initially feel an effort later makes me feel more energised and together again.

Another less obvious resource for listening to others is our personal experiences of pain and suffering. Pain usually has one of two effects on us – either we become stuck in it, bitter perhaps with a chip on our shoulder, or we find ways of integrating it into our experience so that we emerge the more mature and whole. Paul recognised the potential of our own sufferings as being, ' . . . that we can comfort those in any trouble with the comfort we ourselves have received from God' (2 Corinthians 1:4). Mary Craig, whose son Paul was born with Hohler's Syndrome, a rare disease, wrote:

> The value of suffering does not lie in the pain of it, which is morally neutral – but in what the sufferer makes of it. Two people can go through the same painful experience, one be destroyed by it, the other achieve an extra dimension. The real tragedy of suffering is the wasted opportunity.[33]

The 'wasted opportunity' is that of growing into compassion. And it is that com-passion, or suffering with, that many long for as they seek a listener's ear. It is often those who have suffered and found a way of integrating their suffering who are the best listeners to others.

Yet all these resources could be of superficial value without the supreme resource of God himself. In listening to people we can, at best, be available for them to share with us. It is God who is the healer. Our part is so to be centred in him that the person somehow knows she is in a climate of healing. As listener I need to spend time with God listening to him, looking to him, learning to think his thoughts after him, discovering his perspective on people and their situations. In the midst of a full and busy life, I find I need regular times of standing back in order to advance again with adjusted perspective and clearer vision. Each month I try to keep one day clear for this when I can spend longer reading the Bible, listening to God concerning current questions or situations, seeking direction for myself and others. It is often at such times that God has 'wakened my ear morning by morning to listen as one being taught' (Isaiah 50:4, 5). Listening to him will open us to his gifts of discernment, knowledge, wisdom and God's words for us and others, bringing fresh perspectives, insights and truths into our everyday lives. We shall learn to discover God's voice amongst the other voices inside and outside ourselves.

André Louf, a French monk, writes:

A lot of people in these days feel the need to be given a word. They are looking for somebody who can deliver such a word, who can stir up the Word within them . . . so we must apply ourselves to the Word with a tremendous desire for it . . . we must really attend to it, assimilate it eagerly and nurture it in our heart.[34]

It is not only the monk or nun who can expect to be given a life-giving word for others, but any of us who open ourselves to listen to and hear Christ, the living Word, who is our deepest resource.

Exercises

Some of these are for personal reflection and others for sharing in twos or in a group.

Chapter 1   Listening as Ministry
1. Can you think of occasions when you experienced being listened to as gift? hospitality? healing?
2. How did you feel being listened to like this?
   You might like to share one of these occasions with someone else who should simply listen with full attention and without interrupting.

Chapter 2   Qualities in the Listener
1. Recall an occasion when someone listening to you included one or more of the six dimensions in a way that contributed something important to you. Try sharing this with someone else who should not interrupt you but listen with full attention. At the end the listener may ask, 'So what was the most important thing you gained from that time?'
2. Which of the six dimensions do you need to learn more about in your own listening?
3. Who, in your experience, has shown you what it means to be a listener of Christian integrity?

Chapter 3   What are we Listening to?
1. What feelings have you been aware of in some of the people you have been with today?
   What feelings have you been aware of in yourself today?
2. What 'theme song' have you noticed in other people lately? (e.g. 'nothing ever goes right for me', 'I'm no good', 'I'm the greatest', etc.)
3. What beliefs about God have you heard in yourself/others recently?

Chapter 4   Some Cautions
1. Can you think of a recent occasion when, instead of listen-

ing, you used words prematurely or inappropriately? What was happening in you as you did this? How might you have responded differently in the circumstances?

2. Can you think of an occasion when someone listening to you kept asking you questions? How did this feel? What might have been more helpful in the circumstances?

Chapter 5 The Process of Listening

1. How do you react to the way Margaret listened to Anne about Auntie Cath?
   How do you feel about the outcome?

Chapter 6 Sensitive Areas

1. How do you feel when other people share their confidences with you – burdened? pleased? tempted to gossip? anxious? flattered? – or find another word that fits you better. Reflect on a particular occasion when this happened.

2. How would you spell out what you believe about keeping other people's confidences?

3. Have you ever been in a listening situation where you felt out of your depth? What did you do? What else might you have done?

4. 'Maturity in relationships is not about dependence or independence but rather our inter-dependence which recognises that each of us is to give to *and* receive from others'. What do you think of this statement and how have you found it working out in your own experience?

Chapter 7 Resources for Listening

1. List those events, people, places, work, experiences, personal patterns, etc. which resource you.
   List those events, people, places, work, experiences, personal patterns, etc. which drain you.
   In the light of these two lists, reflect on whether you are living a sufficiently resourced life at present.

References

1. Henri Nouwen, *Reaching Out* (Collins, 1976), p. 69.
2. John Powell, *The Secret of Staying in Love* (Argus, 1974), p. 140.
3. Paul Tournier, *A Listening Ear* (Hodder & Stoughton, 1986), p. 32.
4. Henri Nouwen, *op. cit.*, p. 88.
5. R. R. Carkhuff, *Helping and Human Relations: A Primer for Lay and Professional Helpers* (Holt, Rinehart & Winston, 1969), vol. 1, p. 1.
6. Michael Jacobs, *Swift to Hear* (SPCK, 1985), p. 124.
7. For further teaching and exercises, see M. Jacobs, *Swift to Hear*.
8. Gilbert K. Chesterton, *St Francis of Assisi* (Doubleday Image Books, 1957), p. 101.
9. Alastair V. Campbell, *Rediscovering Pastoral Care* (DLT, 1981), p. 105.
10. Michael Jacobs, *Still Small Voice* (SPCK, 1982), pp. 86–7.
11. Alastair V. Campbell, *op. cit.*, p. 12.
12. Gordon Allport, *The Individual and his Religion* (New York, Macmillan, 1950), p. 90.
13. Alastair V. Campbell, *op. cit.*, p. 16.
14. Theophan the Recluse in Igumen Chariton, *The Art of Prayer*, ed. Timothy Ware (Faber & Faber, 1966), p. 98.
15. Henri Nouwen, *The Living Reminder* (Gill & MacMillan, 1982), pp. 30, 31.
16. Blessed Sacrament Fathers, Brackkenstein Community, Holland, *Rule for a new brother* rev. edn (DLT, 1986), pp. 19–20.
17. Alastair V. Campbell, *op. cit.*, p. 104.
18. Michael Jacobs, *Still Small Voice*, p. 30.
19. H. Williams CR, *The Joy of God* (Mitchell Beazley, 1979), p. 70.
20. *ibid.*, p. 71.
21. Paul Tournier, *op. cit.*, p. 14.

22. Michel Quoist, *Prayers of Life*, 'The Telephone' (Gill & Son, 1963), p. 15.
23. Dietrich Bonhoeffer, *Life Together* (SCM Press, 1954), p. 87.
24. For further reading on the use of questions see Michael Jacobs, *Still Small Voice*, pp. 32, 52, 59, 81–2 and *Swift to Hear*, pp. 50–2; Richard Nelson-Jones, *Practical Counselling Skills* (Holt, Rinehart & Winston, 1983), pp. 74–80.
25. Maria Boulding, *The Coming of God* (SPCK, 1982), p. 7.
26. See also Michael Jacobs, *Swift to Hear*, especially sections 3 and 4 on 'Guidelines for Responding' and 'Putting the Guidelines Together'. Some of these guidelines relate closely to what I describe here and are very helpful for practising listening skills.
27. As far as I am aware, the process of mirroring was developed by Eugene Heimler, *Survival in Society* (Weidenfeld & Nicolson, 1957).
28. Joyce Huggett, *Listening to Others* (Hodder & Stoughton, 1988), p. 234. The whole of ch. 11, 'One Spoke of the Wheel', is useful here.
29. See Michael Jacobs, *Still Small Voice*, ch. 8 'Meeting Resistance'; John Powell, *Why am I afraid to tell you who I am?* (Fontana, 1969), ch. 5 'Human Hiding Places'. Also, for use in counselling situations, Richard Nelson-Jones, *op. cit.*, pp. 104–7.
30. S. M. Jourard, *The Transparent Self*, rev. edn (Van Nostrand Reinhold, 1971), p. 6.
31. Eugene Kennedy, *On Becoming a Counsellor* (Gill & Macmillan, 1977), p. 57.
32. Patsy Kettle, *Staying Sane under Stress* (Grove Books, Pastoral Series, no. 31, 1987); Gordon MacDonald, *Ordering your Private World* (Highland Books, 1985); John Sanford, *Ministry Burnout* (Arthur James Ltd, 1984).
33. Mary Craig, *Blessings* (Hodder & Stoughton, 1979), p. 140. See too Alastair V. Campbell, *op. cit.*, ch. 4 'The Wounded Healer'.
34. André Louf, *Teach Us to Pray* (DLT, 1974), pp. 41, 42.

Section 3

Listening to the World

Introduction

Almighty and everliving God,
Whose Son Jesus Christ healed the sick
and restored them to wholeness of life;
look with compassion on the anguish of
   the world,
and by your healing power
make whole both men and nations.
(ASB Collect, 8th Sunday before Easter)

Six years after joining the staff of St John's Theological College, I began to feel restless. Perhaps listening to the world from the protected environment of a college campus had, in part, blunted my understanding of what was going on further afield. The chance to go to Liverpool and work for six months with a church in an Urban Priority Area certainly jolted me into hearing a side of life that was new and disturbing and yet which I could not – and did not want to – avoid.

I arrived in Netherley on Sunday 27 January 1980. A pall of thick, murky fog hung around the eight-storey tower blocks which loomed up into the skies like menacing giant sentinels. My perspective was doubtless exaggerated but I had never been in an area like this before. Each layer of flats was linked by open, draughty corridors – concrete streets in the sky. Even on first acquaintance it struck me that housing was meant to be for people. I had not yet seen the more pleasant council houses but the flats looked inhuman. I parked my car outside Christ Church – it looked rather like a warehouse – and walked along the block, passing 'the mobile' with its tired-looking food for sale. Strange, I thought, a cut loaf is more expensive here than in the South. I was already meeting the unfairness of an outer housing estate with shops so restricted or far away that people were at the mercy of the mobile shops with their high prices. A warm welcome from the vicar's family, tea together and a cheerful service with a small group of believers were more reassuring and I could put aside the questions – at least for the first night.

I soon learnt to listen with my eyes as well as my ears as I visited people in the flats. Burst pipes were a frequent occurrence, as was the lengthy time people were kept waiting by the Council for repairs. The lifts were generally broken, the front doors locked and bolted – hardly surprising in view of the vandalism. Often as the children came out of school, I heard the tinkle of glass as more windows were broken – there were no play areas nearby. Fresh graffiti appeared on the walls overnight and youngsters often used their energies to strip and break the few young trees on the estate. Some days – as when I came across the charred and smoky remains of a settee on one of the corridors – I felt as though all my senses were picking up the malaise felt by many on the estate. Not surprisingly, most elderly people were too scared to go out much for fear of being attacked. And when this happened witnesses were very reluctant to help the police with evidence. Indeed, even near neighbours often did not know each other, isolated as they were in their flats. If they wanted to go into town, buses were few and far between, so taxis were used, adding to the expense and isolation of living.

David Sheppard and Derek Worlock, leaders of the Anglican and Roman Catholic Churches in Liverpool, wrote of this sort of estate:

> The new constructions appeared to have forgotten local culture: the need for ease of communication between people whose strength had been neighbourliness and mutual concern . . . Stacked one above another, their need to communicate was severely thwarted. The higher the high-rise, generally speaking, the less the communication . . . the sheer scale was inhuman. Housing policies are not simply arguments between one ideology and another. Housing is for people.[1]

Yet if the flats were inhuman, the inhabitants were certainly not. As I got to know them individually, I found I was increasingly listening not only with my ears and eyes but also with my heart. There was Bert, long since unemployed, meandering through each day, his small children and the dog running circles around him. Although there was a rule of no pets in the flats, no one seemed to worry too much. Four-footed friends compensated in some small way for the lack of human friendship. On the Sunday I went to Bert and Jean for dinner, we had a whole leg of roast lamb – they couldn't afford it but their generosity was not going to be restricted by their means. Then there was Janet, a lonely single parent who had never before invited another person in for a meal. In a tiny cupboard in her bedroom she had cleared space for a stool, a poster with a Bible verse on it and a candle – an oasis of love and joy where she could pray. Then there was Elsie, mentally ill yet with a great sense of humour – there was a vulnerability about her which tugged my heart. Somehow I heard in her what might happen to any of us put into a stressful environment. There was also Myra, a widowed mother of teenage daughters who, through her relationship with God and the church family, not only found strength to cope but went on to become a respected and loved leader in the church and a JP in the community.

Listening with the heart can be a mixed blessing and, in order not to be at the mercy of feelings, I also had to learn how to listen with my mind and identify the issues that lay behind human faces. Before enforced rehabilitation had taken place with people being removed from the city centre to these outer estates, it was generally agreed that the slum conditions in the city needed to be tackled. Between 1966 and 1973, 33,000 houses were demolished and the flats built to replace the homely back-to-backs. So people lost out on what was certainly unideal but which at least provided what the flats did not – a sense of belonging and community. Some of the people were remarkable in their optimism, humour and warm-hearted resilience, yet they also found themselves trapped in an unjust system and were generally voiceless to deal with it. In the name of progress they became captives not only to inhuman housing but also to blatantly unchristian values. Sheppard and Worlock wrote:

> Sometimes definable groups can be seen to be excluded from the good opportunities of God's world . . . When that is apparent, the Church must make clear where it stands. There is need for responsible intervention in favour of the disadvantaged, for a willingness, if necessary, to give public expression in favour of a voice which otherwise cannot make itself heard. But if that intervention is truly to reflect the needs of the disadvantaged, there must be some genuine listening.[2]

These two Church leaders have certainly set a high standard of genuine listening to their city. They are constantly bringing Christian values to bear on what emerges as they listen to trade unions, the unemployed, the black community, the young people, local government, commerce and industry. So, on the issue of unemployment, they are clear about the facts (Merseyside as a whole had 19.7 per cent unemployment in 1988 though in each of its Urban Priority Areas the percentage was considerably higher) but they also hear very clearly the feelings that are an inevitable part of those facts. They tell of one wife and mother in Kirkby who said, 'I have lived with unemployment for ten years. My husband's pride is now at rock-bottom. He is 42 and feels that he is on the scrap heap. He's very talented but he can't use most of his talents, because they cost money. As a wife and mother of five kids, I'm driven desperate trying to sustain a family.'[3]

This sort of listening involves both heart and head and calls for a constant application of biblical principles and teaching to what is being heard. Therefore it is costly. Yet the alternative is to stop our ears and close our eyes to what is happening around us and, in so doing, to abandon responsibility for our neighbour. In his parable on the sheep and the goats, Jesus pronounced a curse on those who, when he was a stranger, gave him no home, when naked did not clothe him and when in prison did not visit him. In amazement his hearers asked him when such things had happened and he replied, 'anything you did not do for these, however humble, you did not do for me' (Matthew 25:31–46). One sin for which we shall individually and collectively be held responsible is that, when given the opportunity, we chose not to hear the cries of injustice and hurt around us. In stopping our ears to the homeless and unemployed and underprivileged, we were stopping our ears to Christ.

In listening to certain environments with our ears, eyes, heart and mind, we can become overwhelmed or paralysed unless we also listen with the hope that Christ brings. David Sheppard and Derek Worlock, at the end of their book, list what for them have been signs of hope, small yet pointing to the possibility of greater things. And, as I began to open myself to listen to Netherley, so I recognised, amidst much that was wrong, small but real signs of hope:

— the Netherley Christian festival, providing a week of fun, colour and celebration
— the generosity of those who, however poor themselves, would give cheerfully to others in need
— a vicar weeping over the needs of his people
— a vicar's wife helping people learn how to manage their money and them responding
— a local doctor's dedication as he worked long hours in poor conditions
— the resilience of many who would not allow constant disappointments to grind them down
— Protestants and Catholics processing together through the housing estate on a wet, grey Good Friday and standing around the cross to sing, pray and worship
— the growth of individual Christians so that some became lay leaders of great calibre
— a growing congregation discovering and using their God-given gifts so as to become salt and light in the area

Most of the tower blocks have now been demolished and the

rebuilding programme includes new houses and bungalows. I
am glad to have been there when I was and to have seen how
God was working.

I now live in a place very different from Netherley, a village
in the South East of England. Each morning I hear birds singing, a lusty cockerel crowing, a friendly donkey braying.
Nearby is the riverside Red Lion Inn, built in the sixteenth
century and the old Clock House, once a grammar school, its
clock still beautiful with blue face and gold figures. The River
Lea meanders through grassy banks whilst fathers and sons sit
fishing. I feast my eyes on an eighteenth century walled garden
with its variety of trees – the gnarled old pear tree, the stately
giant oak, the dark cypress and the spreading chestnut – and
its abundance of flowers – scarlet geraniums, delicate blue
lobelia, purple and red fuchsias and cheerful snapdragons,
orange, white, pink and sherbet yellow. I hear the children
playing in the recreation ground nearby, safely away from the
main street.

I listen with my heart as well as my ears to the older villagers,
some of whom have been here for fifty to sixty years and have
rich memories to share with those who have time to listen. Jim
and Sylvia can remember the barges laden with grain or gravel
being pulled up the River Lea by horses walking along the tow
path. They remember community events like the concerts given
by the Women's Institute choir at the village hall, the club
where the men congregated for snooker, the village Post Office
and street corners where villagers met to exchange news. Two
world wars drew the village together even closer as people
learnt to care for and support each other. There is still a strong
sense of belonging – it is their village. And even though the
arrival of housing developers with their smart estates has
brought a new generation of young people, the older ones have
not been uprooted and rehoused with all the trauma that can
bring. Jim still listens with thanksgiving to the heartbeat of the
place where he has lived for most of his life. 'I like to go up
the hill at the back,' he said, 'and look across the village. God
has done so much for us. You see the different colours and at

night you see the lights in the village glittering like stars. It's my home.'

Of course there are other aspects of the village that are less picturesque – the increase of traffic, the tensions that inevitably arise between the old and the new, the decline of local industry and shops – but human need is certainly not on the same blatant scale as in Netherley. There are no streets in the sky, no flats with broken lifts, comparatively little vandalism. Yet there is still human need. Stress, fear, pain, loneliness, prejudice and injustice are around for those with ears to hear even if far less obvious. The temptation is to live individualistically and not listen for those needs which are there, sometimes just below the surface.

We start listening to the world by beginning exactly where we are. We may be in a deprived or an affluent area. The important thing is to begin tuning in to what is around us, using not only our ears but also our eyes, our heart, our mind and conscience to hear the good and the bad, the beautiful and the ugly that make up people's lives. And having started, we begin to hear and identify issues arising from our context which beg questions and which lead us on to a wider listening to what is happening in the nation, the world and the universe. These are the contexts we shall consider in this section.

1

Listening to the Structures

If we have begun to listen to our immediate surroundings with every part of us rather than just our ears, then we have already begun to hear the many voices of the world. And before long we shall find ourselves listening to some of the issues emerging from the social structures in which we and others are involved. It was as I got to know people in the Netherley tower blocks that issues of housing, community and belonging became pressing, and as I got to know unemployed people that issues of helplessness, power and the distribution of resources struck me. As I began to hear the issues so I also saw how they affected people. And that in turn raised questions about the structures. If housing is for people, why build dwellings that inhibit the development of community and belonging? And if we believe that work is part of our birthright, why are so many government supported research and development agencies reluctant to be situated in the North rather than the South?

Sometimes the questions felt far too big and the temptation was to put them aside, bury my head in the sand and tell myself there was little I could do to change things. Moreover, if I thought too much, I began to feel guilty. During my Liverpool stay I lodged 'up the hill' whilst those with whom I worked lived 'down the hill'. I had a paid job that I enjoyed whilst every day I was meeting people who didn't enjoy their work, or, worse still, had no job at all. Feelings of powerlessness, guilt and anger sometimes depressed me, especially as I prepared the Sunday sermon for Christ Church, Netherley. What could I say that did not sound hypocritical or 'better than thou'?

One day I took off in the car to North Wales. If only I could get away for a quiet day and be alone with God I might be able to forget the questions and even the people – for a while at least. Clarry, the vicar, knew I was beating a retreat but wisely did not stop me. I walked, breathing in the fresh sea air and tried to forget the questions. The lambs and crying gulls, and white snow-capped hills felt safe. Yet soon the nagging questions returned, 'Is God more here than there?' 'Does he care about Dick who's been jobless for years now? And Jean with her walls running with damp and the Council not lifting a finger to help? God – why don't you *do* something?!' I heard myself shouting into the air. Teaching students about the Kingdom of God felt far safer than this crash course in helping bring it in amongst people enmeshed in social structures that were wounding and belittling.

God didn't appear to be answering my questions that day but, shortly after, I copied out these words into my journal:

> Leave God to act and abandon yourself to him. Let the point of the knife and the needle work. Let the brush of the master cover you with a variety of colours which seem only to disfigure the canvas of your soul . . . *keep to the line of your own advance* and without knowing the details or the map of the country, name and directions of the land you are passing through, *walk blindly along that line* and everything will be indicated to you . . . *Seek only the Kingdom of God* and his justice in love and obedience and all the rest will be given you. (my italics)[4]

Whether I could *do* anything at Netherley, especially short-term, and see fruit for my labours became a less pressing question than getting on with what I was asked to do. Gradually and with help I began:

— to *listen* to the issues arising from the context and structures around me
— to *see* how those structures were affecting people
— to *ask* questions about the structures
— to *discern* what could be my own Christian response

I felt ill-equipped for the task but the alternative was to avoid the pressing questions. I might or might not be able to contribute something but at least I could begin to respond rather than be paralysed with guilt or think there was nothing I could do in the face of so many needs. 'Thy kingdom come' began to feel less like a devout and dutiful prayer and more like an invitation to move into risky territory. Listening to the structures started to become a new and challenging dimension. My only regret was that I had not begun sooner.

But in what other ways are people learning to listen to the world through the structures in which they find themselves? Sarah is a Christian consultant gynaecologist. One issue she hears emerging from her working context concerns position, rank and professionalism. The medical job structure is a pyramid one where there is competition to get to the top. As a consultant she has reached the top of the pyramid. But how does being there affect her and others? 'Others expect you to behave as if you're on a pedestal – indeed it makes them feel safe. If you behave in any other way it can stir up uncertainty for other people.' And yet balancing on a pedestal can, and often does, encourage eccentric and egotistical behaviour, giving the impression that one is beyond criticism. How would we want to question this sort of professional structure? Sarah says of it, 'The trouble is it can leave you impervious to change because you've ceased to hear what others are saying. The patient can't criticise you to your face nor the staff. The traditional model says "the consultant is never wrong" and this militates against learning and change. Yet, in such a position of power there can also be great loneliness and vulnerability. You receive little affirmation from colleagues for the system is not built to provide it.'

It is easy, particularly for an outsider, to want to challenge such power structures which may be an accepted part of the hospital world where everyone understands the rules of the game but is a dubious model of maturity. Where does it leave a Christian whose model of leadership and authority as seen in Christ reverses all notions of pedestals and positions? And where does it leave the consultant outside the hospital structure?

Bruce Rumbold writes:

> Professional understanding enables us to rationalise away criticism or confrontation which might otherwise awaken us to an inner inadequacy and pain. . . . for a professional to be a 'wounded healer' . . . that professional must continually be challenged by something which can neither be mastered nor fended off by his professional attitudes and techniques.[5]

He goes on to plead that the professional has other sorts of relationships – family and friends – of the kind where 'he is challenged as well as consulted, reproached for his failings as well as praised for his virtues, affirmed for himself and not merely for his professional actions'. Indeed, it is only in such 'relationships based on love' that a professional can 'continue to encounter his shadow side and maintain the balance which will permit emotional and spiritual growth for both himself and his patients'.

Seeing the dangers of the pedestal, how is Sarah not only questioning the structure but also discerning her own Christian response? Firstly, she is becoming alert to 'pedestal symptoms' by learning to listen to herself. 'If I simply continue without listening to myself, I become completely impossible both inside and outside the hospital.' Secondly, she is deliberately letting her Christian thinking inform and challenge her professional roles and relationships. Thirdly, she is making time and space for 'relationships based on love'. Once a month she meets with two Christian friends in a mutual support group where, in a disciplined and confidential way, they listen to each other about aspects of their lives where each needs understanding, clarification, prayer, support. It may be a relationship difficulty that is aired, or a fear, or uncomfortable feelings or criticism received. It is very different from chatting with friends. When one is sharing, the other two are listening in a disciplined way and helping the person to hear herself, to identify and clarify the feelings and issues arising. Sarah describes what she has been able to take from her support group to her professional world as of 'huge benefit especially in terms of growing self-understanding'.

It would be easy to think that someone in Sarah's position can more readily listen and respond to the structures than someone at the bottom of the pyramid with no power or influence. But that is not always so.

Kevin, an accountant, was in prison serving a twelve months' sentence for a financial offence. After his release I asked him what words came to mind as he listened to his prison context. 'Fear and uncertainty', he said. 'Fear of the system, of what happened to us and around us, of what was happening to our families, and uncertainty about when we would be released or moved on and what people in the outside world would make of us. The only certain thing about prison is the uncertainty. You heard coldness, no comfort, no peace. There was constant noise and no getting away from it. That's one of the things I remember – noise everywhere, all hours of the day and night – feet marching around, keys, men shouting and crying, occasionally laughing. You heard those sounds that were the opposite of love – just a coldness, ill-feeling and unhappiness. Some buildings can be seeped in warmth but this was a hard, fearful place.'

What issues arose from his prison context? A basic one concerns the purpose of prison – is it chiefly a place of punishment or rehabilitation? or both? The work of rehabilitation is expensive in terms of time and resources. Most prisoners were allocated work but work with little or no meaning to it is of dubious value. Kevin said, 'I had a relatively good job looking after men's records and their earnings of 25–30p per week. But however hard I worked there was no satisfaction. It had no reality, either success or failure – it was meaningless.'

Most prisoners at some point stop and think, 'Why am I here? How did I get here? Where do I go from here?' Yet there is rarely a chance to explore these basic questions with someone who can help. The staff have little time to listen, even if they wanted to. Kevin remarked that the effect of prison is that 'it makes a man self-centred and introverted'. So what could he do about it, caught up in the system as he was?

One Sunday afternoon in the prison chapel an Irishman came and sat beside him and asked if he could talk. Kevin listened to him – he was expecting his release soon and had to find somewhere to live. The social worker had given him some addresses to write to but he said he could not write and would Kevin help him, which he did. Later, Kevin found himself listening to a prison officer who asked for help and, again, he was able to help him clarify a family matter. Gradually he found more and more opportunities to listen. 'I listened as the only thing I could do,' he said.

He and a few other prisoners formed a prayer group. Each evening between 8.30 and 9.00 p.m. they waited in chapel for anyone who might want to come and talk. They would listen to the man then, forming a circle around him, they prayed for him and listened to God about his need. 'I found myself listening to problems, totally unable to do anything except listen. We listened to the lonely man who was worried about his wife, and the man whose daughter was dangerously ill with a relapse following brain surgery. We prayed and prayed that weekend and she came through the crisis. We listened to the man who hadn't heard from his family for about two years. After ten days he had a letter. Too much happened to be just coincidence. We saw many dark situations turned round.' Gradually, in response to the questions thrown up by the structures, Kevin was discerning that there was something he could do.

As well as the listening, each Sunday morning he began to polish his prison shoes, press his one shirt and the tie he had scrounged and go to the chapel service. About ten to twelve men had been attending but within a few months numbers rose to twenty-four (also wearing pressed shirts and ties) and then to nearly fifty. Kevin saw that God was at work and knew he was being used. 'I was aware of his presence and felt myself almost being pushed along by his Spirit. It was astounding.' He had learnt to listen to his environment and its structures, had felt the effects of them on himself and others, had questioned and thought about them and gradually discerned how to respond and take action. A cynic might think that one man's response was not going to make much difference to the prison system. But it did contribute to the prison chaplain attending a Christian Listener Course, after which we prepared teaching notes for him to use with prisoners, teaching them to listen to people and God.

In a different context, Alan started listening to questions raised by the management structures in which he was working. Part of his job was to effect the closing down of a business, including sacking its staff by what he described as 'ruthless methods'. For him this raised disquieting questions about putting profitability before people. Did he want to continue in that working context or not? As he pondered the direction he should take he sensed God was leading him out of that job and into administrative work in a Christian college.

Some, like Janet, find that questions raised by their social context are leading into a further involvement. She first saw real poverty and deprivation when she worked in a day nursery in Scotland. Later, after training as a nurse, marrying and raising children, as she prayed she felt a growing concern for the poor and deprived. She now works as a family assistant in a local Social Services team. The individuals she is helping include Beth, struggling to bring up three boys on £80.55 a week; Jane, with a history of manic depression and agoraphobia who has recently shopped in a supermarket with Janet – the first time in fourteen years; Bill, elderly and almost housebound. 'So many people are left by the wayside,' she said. 'Christ's ministry was to the untouchables and we have many in our own society. I cannot change the system but, as I begin to hear the individuals who live in it, I can begin to make my own contribution. I can bring to the attention of my MP particular examples of injustice; I can keep my eyes and ears open for second-hand clothes, curtains, toys; I can contact various charities for grants towards special items such as holidays; I can ask our church to provide food vouchers for needy families. And I can pray – before I visit people and with silent prayers while I'm there. I

sometimes think perhaps I'm the only one who has ever prayed
for this or that person – particularly the children.' Janet is
listening to issues of poverty, deprivation and injustice within
her context and discerning what she can do.

Sometimes listening to the structures will lead to a hearing
that proves very costly in terms of personal choice. Mark,
seeking entrance to university, was offered sponsorship by a
leading industrial firm involved in communication systems,
radio, etc. It looked an attractive offer. He discovered they
were also involved in building defence systems, which he hesitated about yet concluded that a country needs such resources.
But then came the further discovery that they were also
involved in manufacturing weapons. 'Do I want to work with
a firm that gains money made from destroying others?' He
listened to the questions, heard the implications and discerned
his response – 'No'.

If we are to discover a right social involvement then listening
to and questioning the structures of society is part of our Christian responsibility. The temptation can be to avoid the questions, especially the uncomfortable ones, or run for cover –
sometimes into our Christian churches and fellowships. The
challenge is to engage with what we hear in order to discern
our own response.

John Stott writes,

> In the end there are only two possible attitudes which Christi-
> ans can adopt towards the world. One is escape and the
> other engagement. 'Escape' means turning our backs on the
> world in rejection, washing our hands of it (though finding
> with Pontius Pilate that the responsibility does not come off
> in the wash) and steeling our hearts against its agonised cries
> for help . . . 'engagement' means turning our faces towards
> the world in compassion, getting our hands dirty, sore and
> worn in its service, and feeling deep within us the stirring of
> the love of God which cannot be contained.[6]

Engagement starts with listening and asking questions which,
in turn, lead to the action that is right for each person. For

some it will mean continuing involvement in the structure or system they have come to question and a continuing challenging of it from within. I was only short-term in Liverpool, but Clarry, the vicar, and Sue, his wife, always said, 'We are here for life unless God makes it very clear that we are to move elsewhere'. Their commitment to Church work in an Urban Priority Area is total and they spend much time and energy in listening to and confronting such issues as poverty, housing, injustice, facilities for children. Sarah, the doctor, continues in her hospital role, having identified a leadership model which the medical world upholds yet seeking to work out an alternative Christian one, as Paul taught: 'Don't let the world around you squeeze you into its own mould, but let God re-mould your minds from within, so that you may prove in practice that the plan of God for you is good, meets all his demands and moves towards the goal of true maturity' (Romans 12:1, J. B. Phillips).

For others, like Alan and Janet, listening to the structures may well bring a personal change of direction. For Kevin, listening in new ways in prison and, with others, making a contribution which the prison system did not allow for, means he is now taking fresh ways forward in his work and life. For Mark, listening to value systems different from his own helped him to see more clearly where he stood.

Listening to the structures we live in is one aspect of listening to the world. As we begin to hear and identify issues so we can see the effects they have on people and that, in turn, causes us to ask questions which can help us discern, with God's help, our own involvement and contribution. Whilst this will differ from person to person, for all of us there is the same challenge to open our ears and listen.

2

Listening to the Nation

I have discovered two ways of listening to the news. One is to 'just listen' to what is happening in the nation and world, aware of what is going on yet detached, letting it go in one ear and out the other. I may hear the facts but not their significance. The other way is to listen Christianly, to begin to hear from God's viewpoint and listen with his ears. The picture that had come to me so vividly of the Christ with shrivelled, ineffective ears was a graphic reminder of what we are doing when we are *not* listening Christianly. He seemed to be saying, 'I want people who will listen to each other, to their local community, to my world and to me. I want the ears of my Body to function properly.'

Listening Christianly means listening according to a value system whose origin is the God who loves us and calls us into a Covenant relationship with himself so that we reflect him – his character, values and priorities – in the world. Within this relationship we learn to think as he thinks, feel as he feels, hear and see things as he hears and sees them so that, in listening to events and situations, we stand where he is standing. A Christian listening to world affairs will differ from, say, a materialist. The Christian will see human life and history as held in the hands of God, the natural order as dependent on the supernatural, time as contained within eternity. The materialist will see the world and the natural order as all that there is, with certain consequences that follow from that. What we believe will affect the way we listen and hear. Our beliefs will act as a kind of filter for the information we receive. What values are part of that filter as we watch or listen to the unfolding drama of events in Eastern Europe or the crisis over the ambulance workers' pay dispute, and pray 'Thy Kingdom come on earth'?

At this point we need to take a closer look at our Christian filter of beliefs and values. When we pray for God's Kingdom to come, we are not asking for an earthly or territorial kingdom but for God's kingly reign and rule (already inaugurated by Christ) to come more fully into our lives, both individual and corporate. It is not geographically shaped but heart shaped. We are asking God to establish his reign in us – as Church, nation and world – displacing all that contests his Kingdom and increasing all that demonstrates it.

The Kingdom of God is a central theme in the teachings of Jesus but is not a phrase used by Old Testament writers, though God is often described as 'King'. He is 'King of all the earth' and 'King of the nations' (Psalm 47:7,8). Rather, the Old Testament writers refer to the relationship between God and his people in terms of 'Covenant'. God chose Israel to be in a Covenant relationship of love with himself. For their part, and in loving response, they were to reflect his character – his holiness, faithfulness, kindness, compassion, justice (especially towards the poor and oppressed) – and also his ways – defending the fatherless and widows, loving aliens and providing for their needs, not showing partiality, not accepting bribes, etc. The Israelites were to imitate their God and thus make known his values. They were constantly to remember all he had done for them and, in gratitude, do the same for others.

Central to the character and ways of God are his righteousness and justice. He is: 'A faithful God who does no wrong, upright and just is he' (Deut. 32:4). 'Righteousness and justice are the foundation of your throne' (Psalm 89:14). 'Righteousness' is about rightness, that which matches up to a standard. So God has his standards which are absolutely dependable and which Israel is to reflect. 'Justice' is what needs to be done in a particular situation if people and circumstances are to be brought back into line with his righteousness. Closely linked with these words are two more, 'faithfulness' – God's commit-

ted, unshakeable love – and 'peace' – God's desire for wholeness and harmony at every level. These words describe God's
character and ways and therefore what he wants of his people
in their character and ways – their worship and culture, their
family life and work ethics, their legal practice and treatment
of those in need (there were no Social Services then). Norman
Snaith wrote of God's righteous justice that it 'topples over on
behalf of those in direct need'.[7] No wonder that the writer of
Proverbs says, 'Righteousness exalts [makes great] a nation'
(Proverbs 14:34).

Later in Israel's history it was the eighth century prophets
who proclaimed that living in this way must be the nation's
response to the God who had chosen and set his love upon
them. 'The imitation of God's faithful love, "doing as you have
been done by", is the quintessence of obedience to God's rule.'[8]
As the prophets listened to the nation so they heard, saw and
addressed the people's flagrant departure from God's values of
righteousness and justice. Their reflection of his character had
become not only tarnished but sickeningly distorted. They were
oppressing the fatherless and widows (Isaiah 1:17), accepting
bribes (1:23), depriving the poor of their rights (10:1,2), stea-
ling, murdering and following other gods (Jeremiah 7:9). In
their commerce they were using dishonest scales (Hosea 12:7),
skimping the measure and boosting the price (Amos 8:5),
depriving the poor of justice (5:12), despising and distorting
what was right (Micah 3:9). Their worship and fasting were
hypocritical (Isaiah 58:4) and they were practising sexual
immorality (Amos 2:7). Not surprisingly God tells Isaiah to

> Raise your voice like a trumpet.
> Declare to my people their rebellion
> and to the house of Jacob their sins. (Isaiah 58:1)

What they are doing is abhorrent to God whom Leslie Allen
aptly describes as 'no Olympian, remote from everyday living.
He is the Lord of the shopping centre whose claim over his
people extends to the most mundane of life's duties'.[9] What is
right and just is the 'classic double priority'[10] to which the

prophets are constantly recalling God's people. In their daily
lives they were to reflect his values and priorities. He was to
be seen in all they did.

But to what extent can we apply the value system of eighth
century Middle Eastern God-fearing prophets addressing the
little nation of Israel to our own twentieth century Western
society? And even if many of our own social ills – theft, murder,
sexual abuse, shady business practice, oppression – happen to
be the same as theirs, what about the religious context? Are
we still a Christian nation? Or are we post-Christian?

Christopher Wright helpfully suggests that, rather than thinking in terms of literal imitation, which is not appropriate, we
see the relevance of Israel in terms of paradigm – something
used as a model or example where the basic principle remains
unchanged but the details differ. This approach means that we
do not simply try to apply the social laws of an ancient people
as written to today's world, but neither do we limit their application to historical Israel and say they are totally inapplicable
to either the Christian Church or the rest of the human race.
'If Israel was meant to be a light to the nations (cf. Isaiah 49:6)
then that light must be allowed to illuminate'.[11] He helpfully
looks at how different parts of Israel's social life can act 'as
critique and corrective to analogous aspects of our own age'.[12]
And as to whether we describe our nation as Christian or post-
Christian, it is arguable that, if we have moulded our society
along Judaeo-Christian traditional lines, then it is in order that
we are judged in a similar way to Israel. God hates injustice
and wrongdoing *everywhere* not just in Israel and he wants to
promote justice and righteousness *everywhere*, not just in Israel.
And if we see ourselves as post-Christian and leave God out
of the picture, where else do we look for our standard of what
is right and just?

My intention is not to develop such questions further here
but to say that listening Christianly to the nation will mean
listening according to God's values. Righteousness and justice
were and still are at the heart of his character and ways; these
values were and still are to be reflected in his people.

This double priority of what is right and just is also central to the Kingdom teaching of Jesus. Using the words of Isaiah, Jesus announces his mission as one where he has been sent:

to preach good news to the poor.
. . . to proclaim freedom for the prisoners
and recovery of sight for the blind,
to release the oppressed,
to proclaim the year of the Lord's favour!

(Luke 4:18,19, quoting from Isaiah 61:1, 2)

The good news included word *and* deed, proclamation *and* demonstration. The Kingdom was not only to be taught but also seen. Poverty would not simply be addressed but changed – prisoners (of different kinds) would be set free, blindness (spiritual and moral as well as physical) would give way to sight, the oppressed would be released. Some of these things would happen during Jesus' earthly ministry, some when the Kingdom was fully realised at his return, and some in the interim in which we now live. The Kingdom would not come in a spectacular or showy way but quietly, visible to those with eyes to see. Nor would it come easily but through conflict with the powers of darkness. As well as individuals being affected, so would the patterns and structures of society, some being destroyed but others redeemed by the shalom harmony and wholeness God intended. These things would not be brought about by the high and mighty but often by very insignificant people – the poor in spirit, the meek, the merciful, the peacemakers and those who hungered and thirsted for what was right.

If we are to learn how to listen to the nation and world from God's viewpoint, we need, in response to his love for us, to commit ourselves to his values of righteousness and justice, to put his Kingdom first and to bring him the daily offering of our obedience.

Whilst writing this chapter the ambulance workers are battling for their rights to a proper pay formula, such as the emergency services (fire and police) have. In the early stages of the dispute as I watched the news on TV I tended to half-listen without really hearing – in one ear, out the other – barely registering what was happening except that it all seemed rather inconvenient. Then I consciously tried listening more from God's point of view by applying the criteria of what was right and just. That was quite hard as it involved understanding their pay structure and those of comparable services, the recent distinction between regular ambulance workers and paramedics and asking what is 'right' and 'just' here?

I found that watching the news was greatly helped by listening to Tom, a recently retired local ambulance worker and church member. As he shared I began to see him and his responsibilities in a different light. I listened to his account of the motor bike accident where the rider, still on his bike, was embedded in the back end of an articulated lorry, also his particular horror of cot deaths – he said it often takes him three days to get over one of these. Now, when I listen to the latest news of the dispute, I consciously hold the issue, and particularly the workers, into the God who cares about what is right and just. Resolution of the dispute is not my responsibility, but thoughtful involvement is. Every church is a microcosm of part of the nation and an involvement with each other is greatly enriched as we get to know each other's worlds.

This is certainly true at Holy Trinity, Coventry, where members are learning to listen Christianly to national issues as they hear them represented in their own church and city. Graham Dow became vicar of Holy Trinity, the city centre parish church, in 1981 with a vision for the well-being of the city as well as the church. His first priority was to strengthen and build up the congregation and equip them for ministry and lay leadership. At a clergy meeting, one minister felt God was telling the local churches to concentrate on four particular features of the city – local government, the media, the war legacy and the prevalent materialism. A series of gatherings was arranged to pray for God's light to flood into the city. At the first of these a group of Christians went to the local Council House to pray whilst the rest gathered to listen to God and pray in the church. Later, another group went and stood outside one of the cinemas to pray about the media. On another occasion a large group went to the ruins of the cathedral, burnt down in 1940 in the War, and prayed there. 'We prayed – forgiving the Germans, forgiving God on behalf of the city for what had happened, making sure we had nothing against the Germans. We believe that the legacy of the War is quite a significant feature of the deadness of the city. Its beauty was destroyed then, so we prayed that God would give back the city's creativity. Some people found it an extremely significant time.'

What other features of this Urban Priority Area is the Church learning to listen to and address? Poverty is certainly one. In Coventry there are many who are poor and unable to manage on their income. Graham said, 'The approach of the Government over the last eight to ten years has widened the gap between the rich and the poor and made it harder for the poor. We're having to face that all the time.' The Revd Dr John Vincent, President of the Methodist Conference, recently said that, biblically, a Government is testable by its care of the poor. 'The present Government', Graham said, 'is not good on its care of the poor'. The church started a Sharing Fund to provide help for members who needed more income support than they get, especially single parent families. Food vouchers are given away and they sometimes help those in debt or provide a necessary item, such as a fridge, to a needy family. Three or four years ago 'Meeting Place' began at the Church Centre where, two evenings a week, lonely and needy people could come off the street to talk, eat and belong. The church soon found themselves dealing with problems of accommodation, income and employment. The Centre was, at different times, vandalised but no one said, let's stop this work. Recently the 'Meeting Place' community (about forty regulars) has begun to pray and worship for a good part of its evening session. A satellite church has been born.

The poor now know they are acceptable at Holy Trinity. 'Sometimes our lunch-time Holy Communion is mostly attended by the poor. We have damaged people who walk up and down in the aisles during the service twizzling around. We let them get on with it unless there is a real disturbance. There's a freedom to be who you are. When they know they are welcome, they come, and some of them get healed'.

Colin came from a broken family, was on drugs and drink and loathed himself. 'One day', he said, 'pacing my room, frantic with hunger – 10 days till dole day – I couldn't cope any longer. I cried out, "If there is a God, I could do with some help right now. I hate myself, I can't manage my life – if you exist, help me!" ' He was suddenly filled with a sense of peace though 'no one came round with offers of food or money, and no angels appeared'. But he started to read the Bible, sometimes for hours at a time. About five months later, walking through the city, he heard music coming from Holy Trinity and went in. 'For the first time in my life I met people who just gave love to me. I told them some of the things I had done. They didn't throw me out or hate me but just quietly, patiently loved me. Gradually I came to know Jesus and he is renewing me.' Colin has now completed a City and Guilds course in Caring, works in Coventry as a welder and is a loved member of the church.

The church also worked on the 'Faith in the City'[13] report when it came out. In groups, they took six of its leading chapters, researched them in relation to Coventry and presented their findings to the congregation. They have done something similar with people's jobs, preparing services in groups according to occupation and in the service making a symbolic offering to God of their work. The industry group brought a car into the church!

'In a variety of ways we are teaching the church to listen', Graham said. 'In Holy Week we had three meditations which included a walk around the city centre, returning to church to share what people had heard. We own a building in the city and have been listening to God about how we are to use it. People went there to pray the Kingdom of God into the area and to hear what they thought God might be saying.' Since then plans have progressed – part of the building is to be used as craft workshops and coffee shop and part possibly as a counselling and ministry centre. 'I believe that if we give God an open door, he'll take it and – at the moment when we can, act on it.'

Personal and corporate devotion are meaningless unless their outcome is Kingdom-shaped and they demonstrate God's values of righteousness and justice so that the poor experience salvation, the blind begin to see, the oppressed find release.

Michael Harper wrote:

. . . the Church and the world miss something vital when the voice of the prophet is no longer heard in the land.

We are living in days which are not exactly calculated to encourage the career of a prophet . . . his main function is to 'listen'. The Church today is notoriously bad at listening and being still and quiet enough to do so.[14]

In many vital areas of our national life the Church today lacks a clear prophetic voice. Whilst we can be thankful for David Sheppard and Derek Worlock and their prophetic perspective and example in the inner city, there are other major issues which are not being addressed with authority. May God raise up twentieth century prophets who, as they listen to the nation and to God, will hear his word for the hour and fearlessly pass it on. But may we also be faithful and fearless listeners.

3

Listening to the World

History books will be written about this present era – and make for exciting reading. Even whilst writing this chapter the news is dominated by the release from prison of Nelson Mandela after twenty-seven years in captivity. Several times a day there are moving scenes on the TV screen – his walk, hand in hand with Winnie, from the prison gates to a waiting car, his first speech to thousands of black people, appealing for discipline. 'Go back to your schools, factories, mines, communities. We are going forward – the march towards freedom and justice is irreversible.' Emotions were stirred as he arrived home to a small house he must have wondered if he would ever see again. *And* there was also the reaction of those from the Extreme Right as they marched in protest, waving crudely worded banners.

Shift the focus and other momentous things have also been happening. The Communist Party in Russia has given up the monopoly of power it has held for over seventy years – a watershed in the country's history. *And* Azerbaijan is in a ferment of bloodshed and violence. A distraught Armenian reported how he saw a fellow countryman thrown from a fifth floor apartment – 'they cut up his body into pieces, put them in a bucket and burnt them'. In Berlin there has been great rejoicing as the Wall comes down and families formerly divided are reunited. *And* we also see shots of Bitterfeld in East Germany with its severe industrial pollution, skeletons of trees and fountains of chemicals springing from an underground waste pipe. In Romania we rejoiced at the dramatic overthrow of the Ceausescu regime after a whole country had suffered twenty-four years of total subservience to one man and his wife. *And* we saw the covers removed from some of the horrors he had deliberately chosen to hide from the world – like the hospital for 200 severely disturbed children, most of them naked and playing with their own excrement, some bound in rags to stop them destroying themselves or each other.

To engage with world affairs at present is both absorbing *and* demands a tough constitution. I can sympathise with a friend who wrote to me, 'Sometimes lately the TV news has such horrifying stories of the world I just can't watch. It is a very bewildering place nowadays'. One response is just that – not to watch or read what we cannot cope with, and who can blame the elderly or sensitive person for switching off as a means of self-defence? A similar response is that of helplessness, the feeling that 'I can't do anything about it so I'd better not let it come too close', often accompanied by guilt. Faced with situations of injustice and suffering we want to *do* something – raise money, buy Third World products, use recycled paper – anything to help change the way things are. Charles Elliott calls this the 'stamp-machine' approach and says it is inadequate since it does not deal with the roots of injustice. Another response – one with which I identify – is to insulate ourselves from the world in a privatised and individualistic religion. 'Because I cannot cope with the pain of the world, I substitute myself for the world, and my religion, which will still surely not be painless, is focussed upon *my* relations with God, *my* state of grace, *my* progress (or regress) along the spiritual path.'[15]

I still have the letters I wrote (but never sent) to the Superiors of two Religious Communities asking if I could come and test out my vocation to a life of prayer. I doubt if I would have survived the first month. It took some years to discover that I had written out of a pressing personal need to run away from life and the world. Gradually the root needs of fear and despair were unearthed and identified. They continue to be healed. Even so, I can still recognise myself in Elliott's words:

. . . somehow I have to find the courage to face the fear, to endure the pain, so that in both my prayer life and my active life I can take the world with utmost seriousness. To do less . . . is to deny both the majesty of the Creator and the reality of love incarnate. But watch me: I'll run to that ghetto, so warm, so comfortable, so undisturbed and undisturbing, given half a chance, as long as the pathology is unacknowledged and accordingly untreated.[16]

I have since learnt that nuns with a genuine vocation are not world avoiders but world embracers.

How then do we learn to listen to our world with 'utmost seriousness' without becoming overwhelmed or running away? In the last chapter we saw how listening Christianly means listening to God's values and priorities. In relationship with him we begin to think as he thinks, feel as he feels, hear and see things as he hears and sees them so that, through us, he is reflected in the world. The phrase Paul uses is 'the renewing of your mind' (Romans 12:2). We can either be 'conformed to the pattern of this world' – its standards, values and goals – or we can be 'transformed by the renewing of our mind' so as to become aligned with God's will and purposes. The process whereby we progress from one to the other is described in the New Testament as 'metanoia', a turnabout or change of direction involving mind, heart and action – 'repentance'. And this is a gradual and continuing experience, God acting upon and in us so that we begin to see with his eyes, think his thoughts, adopt his values, incarnate his life. He shares his perspective with us so that the whole of life 'comes under the interpretation of faith'.[17]

In the Bible are not only recurring values such as justice and righteousness which reflect God's character but a world view and historical perspective which reflect his actions and purposes. John Stott describes this in terms of 'the fourfold scheme of biblical history'[18] – Creation, Fall, Redemption and Consummation (or New Creation). It is within this framework of history and belief that we can listen to and hear the world from God's perspective.

i. Creation

God created the world in all its order, diversity, beauty and interdependence as an expression of his love. The climax of his creative activity was his making man and woman in his own image – Godlike – with the capacity for relating to him and to each other, with the power of moral choice, rational, responsible, social, creative. Together they were given dominion over the earth, accountable to God for its care and for sharing its resources.

ii. Fall

Through disobedience and sin their harmony with God and the created world was broken. Every level of relationship was disturbed, between people – family, sex, society, nations, with themselves – intellectually, emotionally, spiritually, physically, and within nature itself. ' "Original sin" means that our inherited human nature is now twisted with a disastrous self-centredness.'[19]

iii. Redemption

Yet God's plan was not to abandon his world but to redeem it. Making a Covenant, first with Abraham then with Israel, he constantly reaffirmed through the prophets that, despite people's sin, his commitment to them and to his Kingdom would continue. With Christ's coming to earth, God's Kingdom came. Here was 'a power that changed lives, reversed personal standards and values, and presented the radical challenge of a new way – God's way – to the fallen structures of power and authority among men.'[20] The cross and resurrection of Jesus was the climax of redemptive history (though not its end). God was identifying with his suffering world. And, as he sent his Holy Spirit, so his power became available and his promises extended beyond Israel to all the world, just as he had promised Abraham.

iv. New Creation

In God's time Christ will return to perfect and fulfil his purposes – the restoration and redemption of God's whole creation. He will raise the dead, judge the world, regenerate the universe and perfect his Kingdom so that righteousness and peace prevail. And this gives us true hope, an optimism which 'without shedding any of the realism induced by a full appreciation of the fall, goes behind it to the will of a good creator and redeemer God, and believes that just as the chaos and brokenness of the fall was not the first word about man and the earth, so it will not be the last word either'.[21]

This then is the biblical framework within which we listen to the world, gain perspective as history unfolds and see God working out his purposes.

> Creation provides our basic values and principles . . . the fall keeps us earthed in the reality of human stubbornness and a world under curse, preserving us from crippling disillusionment. The history, law and traditions of Old Testament Israel, show us how God sought to work out his moral will in a specific context . . . The incarnation brings God alongside us in our struggle, especially with the knowledge of the presence of his Kingdom in the world. The cross brings the power of genuine reconciliation . . . The life and mission of the church keeps our eyes on the corporate nature of God's redemptive purpose . . . Our future hope of the New Creation sets a constant goal before us as a standard for our values and policies, and is the guarantee that our labour is not in vain, for the future belongs to the Kingdom of God.[22]

If this is our framework for seeing from God's perspective, how can we apply it to listening to world events? Richard Foster encourages us to 'meditate upon the events of our time and to seek to perceive their significance. We have a spiritual obligation to penetrate the inner meaning of events and political pressures, not to gain power, but to gain prophetic perspective'.[23]

Many of us have been deeply moved as we watched recent events in South Africa. What had seemed impossible – Nelson Mandela's release from jail after twenty-seven years – was happening before our very eyes. His words, as he walked into prison, had been, 'There is no easy path to freedom', and now here he was, twenty-seven years later, walking out. Prisoner No. 466 64 was now a free man. Meditating on it in the light of our suggested framework, we can see it not simply as a thrilling turn of events in the history of South Africa but also as part of God's ongoing redemptive purposes. Biblically it is clear that God created all people equal. His creation of the human race was an expression of himself – the 'imago Dei' was in every person. God has no favourites. Archbishop Desmond Tutu, during his visit to Birmingham in 1989, told us to think of a piano keyboard with its black and white notes. You can play a tune of sorts if you play black or white alone, but only if you play both together can true harmony be heard. Humans are of infinite worth intrinsically because they are created in God's image. Apartheid, injustice, oppression, exploitation are not only wrong; 'they are positively blasphemous because they treat the children of God as if they are less than His'.[24]

Wambali, a black student from Malawi, told me, 'In Malawi I was always known as happy and laughing. In South Africa I was known as someone who was negative and depressed. I started hating my own blackness – which I'd never done before – then I started hating God'. Tutu reminds us also of the goodness of creation in South Africa:

I come from a beautiful land, richly endowed by God with wonderful resources, wide expanses, rolling mountains, singing birds, bright shining stars out of blue skies, with radiant sunshine, golden sunshine. There is enough of the good things that come from God's bounty; there is enough for everyone, but apartheid has confirmed some in their selfishness, causing them to grasp greedily a disproportionate share, the lion's share, because of their power.[25]

Apartheid, Tutu said, is not only wrong but blasphemous. And this is one of the consequences of the Fall – one that has completely distorted what being a human being, made in God's likeness, is all about. Evil of its very nature involves distortion. The root distortion of apartheid is that it declares people were made for separation, whereas God declares we were made for fellowship, togetherness and interdependence. The foetid atmosphere of this distortion has become a breeding ground for many related evils – enforced population removal with three and a half million people dumped like rubbish in poverty-stricken arid homelands; migratory labour where a father must leave his wife and children in homelands where they eke out a miserable existence while he goes to the white man's town as a migrant worker and lives an unnatural life in a single sex hostel for eleven months of the year; some children as young as eleven years being detained, others killed with rubber bullets, and no one held culpable; improvised housing with inadequate sanitation.

Yet God is there amidst the distortion and evil. He has not abandoned his people but is present redemptively. Some of those he is using are known, public figures but many are unknown and far from the public eye. In one village, church leaders went to keep vigil on the eve of the enforced removal of its people. The churches and schools had already been demolished, the water supply cut and the bus service to the nearest town suspended (so that people should move 'voluntarily'). The home of a village elder was due to be bulldozed the following day and he and his wife and goods transported away. In the middle of the night he got up, went outside and prayed, 'God, thank you for loving us'. A redemptive sign. A young man, now a priest, said, 'When you're in detention and they use their third degree methods on you, you look on them and say, "These are God's children. They're behaving like animals but need us to help them recover the humanity they've lost".' Another redemptive sign.

As I try to listen to the inner meaning of current world events, I pay particular attention to those who are clearly men and women both of prayer and of justice who have 'prophetic perspective' – people like Desmond Tutu, Allen Boesak, Nelson Mandela – who have been tried and tested through persecution and suffering and yet have stood firm for truth. Yet 'it is not just the churchmen who have a monopoly on the word of God. There are other men and women, often unbelievers, who speak with authority about truth and justice. We must be alert, poised like Elijah at the mouth of his cave to catch the Word, and not be fooled into disregarding it because it comes from the mouth of someone whose religion, political stance or cultural background is alien to our own.'[26] Because we are *all* made in God's image, we will hear important insights and truths through each other if we are prepared to listen carefully and with discernment.

The redemptive struggle against evil continues in South Africa. God's desire is for harmony, shalom, reconciliation. He has called his people to be his agents, 'to transfigure the world's ugliness into the beauty of the Kingdom, its hate into the love of the Kingdom, its selfishness into the desire to share the compassion, joy, peace and caring of the Kingdom.'[27]

Its fulfilment is still future, an unknown but certain hope, though glimpses of it are present for those with eyes to see. When Tutu was Dean of St Mary's Cathedral, Johannesburg, he could remember the time when black people would sit on a bench at the back, not coming up for Holy Communion until after the whites. Yet, in the 1970s, he could say:

As I have knelt in the Dean's stall at the superb 9.30 High Mass, with incense, bells and everything, watching a multi-racial crowd file up to the altar rails, . . . the one bread and

the one cup given by a mixed team of clergy and lay ministers, with a multi-racial choir, servers and sidesmen – all
this in apartheid-mad South Africa – then tears sometimes
streamed down my cheeks, tears of joy that it could be that
indeed Jesus Christ had broken down the wall of partition
and here were the first fruits of the eschatological community
right in front of my eyes.[28]

A sign of God's New Creation.

Creation, Fall, Redemption, New Creation – this is the biblical framework we have for listening to the world. And as we
watch and listen to world news it is this framework which can
give us the perspective we need to see and hear and think from
God's point of view.

However, in seeking 'to penetrate the inner meaning of
events' it is not the accumulation of facts that is the goal. I
might arm myself with a vast amount of information about
South Africa or any other part of the world. But what do I *do*
with the facts? How do they affect my attitudes, values, prayer,
actions? Charles Elliott says, 'Know enough, enough to nourish
and sustain and focus, but sit lightly to what is known since it
is as likely to obscure as it is to reveal.'[29] He goes on to describe
another dimension of knowing which he calls 'subjective knowledge' and which complements knowledge of the facts. This is
more of an empathic knowing. It may come through our own
experience of being in certain situations where we not only
accumulate factual information but also experience the facts so
that we know what they feel like. It may also come from
hearing other people's experiences – especially those we know
and respect. I have not yet been to South Africa but have
friends who know the country well. Rick who was imprisoned,
John who was likely to be, Mike who wept his way through his
decision to return there. As I listened to their stories about
themselves, their hopes and fears, their calling to ministry in
the Church, I became involved in ways that were different from
knowing the facts alone. And it was this empathic knowing
which seemed to take things from the head to the heart and

motivate me to feel as well as to think and then to pray from a place of heart involvement.

The third source of this 'subjective knowledge', Charles Elliott says (and the least satisfactory), is the media – the printed word, the film or the news report. Earlier we considered some negative attitudes to world events as they come to us through the media – switch off, succumb to feelings of helplessness and guilt, avoid. But another approach – one used in Ignatian meditation of the Gospels – is to reflect on an event using the imagination to identify with different characters and happenings. Take a news item and prayerfully meditate on it by putting yourself into the scene, asking the Holy Spirit to lead you.

I did this after watching on TV a protest march of the Extreme Right white South Africans shortly after Mandela's release. Many were red-faced and angry and I reacted against them, fiercely critical of the slogans they held aloft on banners – 'Stop integration', 'Continue political segregation'. One of the crowd was carrying a black head on a pole – it looked like a gorilla – draped around with a red cloth resembling blood. Indignation surged up within me. How dare they? Later that day, still burning with anger, I took the scene into prayer. As I thought about the protestors I asked, where would I have been in the scene? Suddenly I saw myself *amongst* them, waving my banner alongside theirs. I felt their tense, surging bodies full of scornful energy. I was full of rage and fear, despising and panic. Suddenly, as I looked up and saw the black head of the enemy on its pole, it seemed to turn into the head of Christ – Christ impaled on a stake – and I was part of the angry mob beneath him crying out, 'Crucify him! Crucify him!' I wept as I realised what was happening – the evil I had recognised and was quick to project on to others was also in *me*.

Being drawn into that kind of prayerful meditation in which I expose myself to the Spirit of truth reveals in me a need for ongoing 'metanoia', an ever-deepening conversion of attitudes, prejudices and values. It was a gift of grace, two days later, to sit with a black African Christian who had suffered some of the indignities of apartheid and see Christ in his open, smiling face. It felt as though the risen Christ was present, forgiving and accepting me. Gerard Hughes wrote:

> Knowing our sinfulness and repenting is a lifelong, continual process. We can never reach a stage before death when we no longer need repentance, because there are layers upon layers of consciousness within us, and each moment of existence can reveal these layers, if we let it, and show us the depth of the tendency within us to refuse to let God be God.[30]

This chapter began with the world out there and we are now into our inner world – a reminder that the two are inextricably linked. It is only when our mind has descended into our heart that true change will come about. It is in that inner place that we can see 'that what is most universal is most personal and that indeed nothing human is strange to us.'[31]

Listening to God's world then means learning to listen and hear from his perspective. The biblical framework of Creation, Fall, Redemption and New Creation shows us his purposes for history and within this framework our listening can take place knowing that, whatever happens, God is committed to the world he made. Creation reminds us of the beauty of the world and the uniqueness of people, made in God's image, so that we listen reverently; the Fall reminds us of evil and its consequences, so that we listen realistically; Redemption reminds us of God's commitment to saving what he has made, so that we listen compassionately; the New Creation reminds us what is yet to come, so that we listen hopefully. And as we listen to world events with our hearts as well as our heads so we discover an inner solidarity with all people which can lead both to their healing and ours.

Once, whilst on retreat, I was trying to pray for some of the needs of the world. As I laboured my way through a mental list of places and events I found myself getting more and more heavy and bogged down with it all. Suddenly a complete change of perspective was given – given in that it was not of my own making. A picture came into my mind's eye of bare feet standing on soil. The feet quite clearly had been wounded. Then the soil seemed to change into a large globe of the world. The wounded feet were still firmly standing on it. As I meditated on them so my gaze travelled upwards and I saw Christ the King, crowned and majestic, robed in light. From this picture three insights came freshly to me – the great multitude from every nation and tribe who will, one day, stand before the throne (Revelation 7:9); the tree of life whose leaves are for the healing of the nations (Revelation 22:2); and the transformation of the Kingdoms of this earth into the Kingdom of God (Revelation 11:15). In that day

The kingdom of the world
　has become the kingdom
　of our Lord and of his Christ,
and he will reign for ever and ever.

4

Cosmic Listening

In the last chapter we were considering the world in terms of the nations. But how do we listen to even wider issues concerning the universe? When we hear of the massacre of rain forests which support half the planet's known living species and affect our weather, how do we react? Or that the use of aerosol propellant gases is causing irreparable damage to the ozone layer? Or that radioactive leaks from power stations can result in untold damage to health, land and livestock as happened at Chernobyl in 1986? How do God's promises of redemption and new creation apply to our universe in the light of the urgent issues we are faced with today? In this chapter we shall use the same biblical framework of Creation, Fall, Redemption and New Creation to guide us in our listening to the whole created order.

i. Creation

Whatever part of the universe we are listening to, it had its origin in God's creative self-expression. 'Creation is God's work of art and he cares deeply for every aspect of it'[32] – the heavens and the earth, light and darkness, dry land and water, plant and animal life, man and woman. Interestingly, many scientists these days are commenting not only on the sense of order and design in the universe but also its beauty and mystery. John Polkinghorne, physicist and priest, sees this as 'a rational response to the strange and beautiful world science discloses, with its feel of "more than meets the eye" '.[33] Perhaps science will not after all be the chief contender to knock down the Christian understanding of the world's origin.

Not only is the Bible unequivocal about the origin of the universe but also the continuing care and concern the Creator has for it. Creation was not a 'hands on, hands off' operation. Ian Bradley writes: 'No longer can God be seen as the remote watch maker in the sky who has wound up the mechanism of the universe and observes it from a distance as it ticks away. Modern science suggests rather a creator and sustainer of all things who is constantly active in the world.'[34]

God's ongoing care for his creation is a recurring theme in the Psalms. He 'renews the face of the earth' (Psalm 104:30), 'cares for the land and waters it' (Psalm 65:9). Jesus taught that the birds of the air are fed by his Father (Matthew 6:26), the lilies of the field adorned by him (6:29), the grass clothed by him (6:30). As I write, it is springtime and there are abundant signs of the renewal of creation in the garden – the bright yellow aconites pushing their way up through the grass again, the delicate sky-blue scillas – more prolific than ever this year, the sticky horse chestnut buds growing fatter by the minute. A new season's growth, a concentration of fresh, surging life and energy which speak not only of beauty and variety but also of the God who created and renews his world.

The Bible also describes the created world as being alive and responsive to its Creator. Not only can humans love and praise God but the trees of the forest sing for joy and clap their hands, the mountains and hills skip like rams, the waters lift up their voice. 'It is almost as though every created being is an instrument in a cosmic orchestra, giving its own distinctive tune to the great symphony that is being played in response to the biddings of the unseen conductor'.[35]

But as well as being part of creation's song of praise, humans are given dominion over God's world (Genesis 1:28). 'Dominion' is about responsible rule – it is not synonymous with domination or destruction. There is no doubt who is creator of the world yet God appoints humans as his deputies, accountable to him for the care and cultivation of his creation. Here is the picture not only of a responsible steward and care-taker but also of a good gardener 'who knows and loves his plants, knows their needs and tends them with the utmost tenderness. . . . Caring for and cultivating the world he created . . . is part of God's plan for mankind and the means by which we reflect his glory'.[36] What then has gone wrong?

ii. Fall

A single day's newspaper this week makes for gloomy reading as far as ecology goes – the River Bourne in Surrey polluted by 5,000 gallons of chemicals resulting in the death of thousands of fish and with the after-effects expected to continue for up to five years; criticism from six countries at the North Sea Conference of Britain's failure to stop immediately the dumping at sea of industrial and sewage waste. The Baxter Report, after two years' study into the outbreak of two cancer clusters in Humberside from which sixteen children have died, notes that workers in heavy industry face exposure to radioactivity levels far higher than those considered safe.[37]

Add to these news items the growing danger of the 'greenhouse effect'. The final statement from the Toronto Conference in 1988 was unambiguous in its warning:

> Humanity is conducting an unintended, uncontrolled, globally persuasive experiment whose consequences could be second only to global nuclear war. The earth's atmosphere is being changed at an unprecedented rate by pollutants . . . These changes represent a major threat to international security and are already having harmful consequences over many parts of the globe . . . It is imperative to act now.[38]

Other environmental crises include de-forestation (a single Sunday edition of the New York Times consumes 150 acres of forest land), acid rain (the UK is Western Europe's biggest culprit for the emission of sulphur dioxide) and the continuing threat of ultimate environmental disaster – nuclear holocaust. The temptation is to distance ourselves from the facts and hope that 'they' (that is the scientists, industrialists, politicians) will do something to stop it all. But that is not good enough. For we are *all* involved in responsible stewardship of the earth. We are *all* involved in the cosmic dilemma.

In his 1989 Richard Dimbleby Lecture, 'Living off the Land', the Duke of Edinburgh ended by quoting the words of an Indian tribal leader in the Western United States who, nearly 140 years ago, wrote:

> This we know: the earth does not belong to
> man; man belongs to the earth.
> Whatever befalls the earth befalls the sons
> of the earth.
> Man did not weave the web of life; he is
> merely a strand in it.
> Whatever he does to the web, he does to
> himself.

Was this, the Duke asked, the end of living and the beginning of survival?[39]

With amazing prophetic insight and long before our misuse of the elements assumed its present proportions Hildegard of Bigen (1098–1179) warned:

> I heard a mighty voice crying from the elements of the world: 'We cannot move and complete our accustomed rounds as we should do according to the precepts of our Creator. For humankind, because of its corruptions, spins us about like the sails of a windmill . . . now we stink from pestilence and from hunger after justice'.

She went on to prophesy:

> As often as the elements of the world are violated by ill-treatment, God will cleanse them through the sufferings and hardships of humankind . . . All of creation God gives to

humankind to use. But if this privilege is misused, God's justice permits creation to punish humanity.[40]

How are we as Christians listening and responding to these huge challenges? I was thinking about Hildegard's prophecy as I walked along the local river path. The previous week there had been gale force winds. Some of the trees, sprouting new buds, had been uprooted and thrown to the ground. Others, still standing, had branches broken, hanging down like fractured limbs. As they creaked and sighed in the cold wind I was reminded of Paul's word, 'We know that the whole creation has been groaning as in the pains of childbirth right up to the present time. Not only so, but we ourselves who have the first-fruits of the Spirit groan inwardly as we wait eagerly for our adoption as sons, the redemption of our bodies' (Romans 8:22,23).

The groaning is about the 'frustration' (v. 20) and 'bondage to decay' (v. 21) which both the created world and we ourselves experience. It has its roots in sin – that pride, lust and greed whereby we put our own gods at the centre rather than the living God. E. F. Schumacher sees our contemporary god to be:

> . . . the prevailing religion of economics which sees the primary meaning and purpose of human life in the limitless expansion of every man's needs . . . his craving for more and more material satisfaction . . .
>
> We cannot continue to deify economic progress in purely quantitative terms . . . if it is not to lead to disaster it must be progress according to a new pattern inspired by a profound understanding of, and deep reverence for, our natural environment which is not man-made but God-given.[41]

Yet, whilst we are clearly responsible for our own priorities and their consequences, there is a further dimension also. Paul writes about warfare with the unseen but equally real world. He tells the Ephesians to:

> be strong in the Lord and in the strength of his might. Put

on the whole armour of God, that you may be able to stand against the wiles of the devil. For we are not contending against flesh and blood, but against the principalities, against the powers, against the world rulers of this present darkness, against the spiritual hosts of wickedness in the heavenly places. (Ephesians 6:10–12 RSV)

So our struggle includes another level beyond the environmental. It 'is not with humans but with cosmic intelligences; our enemies are not human but demonic'.[42] They are powerful, wicked and cunning, bringing hostility, fear and bondage to God's world. Although some modern commentators believe Paul was referring simply to human power structures, the New Testament is unambiguous that the principalities and powers are supernatural agents of darkness, used by Satan to undermine the activity of God. Failure to recognise these is failure to engage in a battle which extends beyond the material to the spiritual realm and for which God has provided both offensive and defensive weapons (Ephesians 6:13–18). Our part is to listen, discern and engage, using the shield of faith, the sword of the Spirit, which is the Word of God, and prayer. Many monks and nuns are practised in this as they pray, often in the dark hours of the night, against 'the snares of the enemy'. One contemplative order of nuns prays every night between 2.00 a.m. and 3.00 a.m., a time when those awake or in despair can be at their lowest point and especially vulnerable to the powers of darkness. We have much to learn from them about cosmic listening and prayer.

Yet the good news is that, although the skirmish continues, the victory has already been decisively won through the redeeming and reconciling work of Christ who on the cross 'disarmed the principalities and powers . . . triumphing over them' (Colossians 2:15). If fallenness has affected the whole cosmos, so too will redemption.

iii. Redemption

Just as God is at work redemptively amongst the nations, so he is in the whole cosmos. His love is not limited to human beings but extends beyond them to all that he made. 'God so loved the world [cosmos] that he gave his one and only Son' (John 3:16). 'God was reconciling the world [cosmos] to himself in Christ' (2 Corinthians 5:19). 'Christ is before all things, and in him all things hold together . . . God was pleased to have all his fullness dwell in him, and through him to reconcile to himself all things, whether things on earth or things in heaven, by making peace through his blood, shed on the cross' (Colossians 1:17–20). Here is the Christ who saves, redeems and reconciles the fallen cosmos.

In Romans 8:19–23 Paul points out that just as there is an integral link between our own sufferings and those of the whole creation so there also is between our redemption and that of the whole creation. Whilst Christ's redemptive work is unique, we are to co-operate in God's plan to redeem and reconcile the cosmos. Part of our being made in his image is to join him in his creative and re-creative work. So 'by working with nature rather than exploiting it, by treating it with reverence and awe rather than arrogant contempt . . . we are helping that mysterious process of cosmic redemption.'[43]

But how can this work out in practice? Each of us needs to discern our own response to these huge issues. For some of us, it might be to become more informed about and add weight to local or national initiatives which protect the environment. For others it might mean being more careful to use re-cycled and 'environment friendly' products such as aerosols without CFCs or chlorine-free bleach. I want to give three further examples of learning to listen and co-operate with God in his redemptive plans for the universe.

The first is about Peter and Phyllida who, with their three sons, were living full and busy lives in the south of England when, one day, Phyllida saw a book whose title *How then should we live?* stuck in her mind. 'Surely Christians shouldn't drift along in life driven by circumstances? . . . So I set aside a day of quiet for prayer and fasting, hoping that the Lord would speak to me and show me his will for our lives . . . he showed me an overall view that almost took my breath away, and yet everything within me agreed that it was right and wanted to shout for joy.' She wrote down three lists – Christian objectives (to be a light in the world, a loosely knit community, a place of retreat and healing, etc.), lifestyle objectives (to live simply, sharing all things and being available to listen to people, etc.) and ecological objectives (to conserve the environment, to 'have dominion' by exercising loving responsibility over living things, etc.).

Six years (and much faith-stretching) later, Peter and Phyllida discovered in the Gwaun Valley near the Pembrokeshire coast the stone farm buildings that were to become Ffald-y-Brenin (Sheepfold of the King). Gradually the ground was tended and the buildings restored. Many times they prayed and, in 1988, it was opened as a centre of retreat and refreshment. The simplicity and beauty of the place are remarkable – the grey stone buildings blending with the muted shades of the valley, the purple heather garden and waterfall glinting in the sun, the renewed woodland, millpond and vegetable garden – many living examples of working *with* rather than against nature. Minnie, the large, contented cat, was found wild and starving, living in a drain and not allowing anyone to touch her. Now she purrs with affection and responds to touch and love. Gracie, the elderly nanny goat, was like a skeleton and on her last legs when she arrived four years ago. She now has a new lease of life as have the four Jacob's sheep (previously unwanted) who like being within sight of the house and are always ready to eat out of your hand. 'We take in all unwanted things and they thrive', said Phyllida.

As I sat, early one sun-filled morning, on a grey boulder high on the hillside in a field sparkling with dew, drinking in the gentle and healing silence of the place, I experienced freshly the harmony and beauty of God's world – a sign of creation redeemed.

A second example comes from Netherley, the urban overspill area described earlier. Amongst the grey tower block flats and dark concrete pavements, a few spindly trees stood, solitary reminders of the created world. But they were often stripped and broken by the local children who had no recreation ground there. The vicarage garden, fenced but easy to enter, also boasted a few trees and plants which, like those on the estate, were periodically uprooted or removed. Yet when this happened Sue, the vicar's wife, would quickly put in new seedlings and plants, renewing what had been spoilt and broken. If the flats reflected little of God the Creator, then at least a garden used by church members could be a sign of creation redeemed.

A third example, also from Netherley, illustrates how some of the church family began to engage with cosmic principalities and powers in spiritual warfare. We experimented with prayer walks as an expression of joining with God in his desire to redeem a dark area. In twos we walked, without discussion, around the corridors of the flats, keeping the Name of Jesus in our hearts, opening our eyes and ears to our surroundings and praying silently for people and places. As we returned afterwards to the church, some would report 'a darkness outside number –' or a feeling that 'we had to pray for what was going on in number –', or experiencing 'a sadness about number –'. Sometimes the church leaders knew of the abuse or marital anguish or occult practices that were going on inside those flats. In such ways we learnt together that the battle we were engaged in and the powers we prayed against were real and that the redeeming work of Jesus was needed salt and light for the estate.

iv. New Creation

'God's direct control of affairs, which is what the Kingdom means, is strictly unimaginable. Humanity has dreamed of it and does so still, but the dreams are partial glimpses only.'[44]

I sensed I had such a dream as I walked one afternoon with

a friend on Egton High Moor in North Yorkshire. The weather was bleak and stormy yet with sporadic gleams of pale light. Across the moors in the distance were the three giant 'golf balls' – the early warning system at Fylingdales. They have always struck me as sinister, reminders of a complex network of underground nuclear defence activity. Suddenly, as we stood looking at the beauty of the moors and the disturbing 'golf balls', a colourful, bright rainbow appeared, arching over and enclosing the whole Fylingdales area. Would all that it represented of nuclear energy be redeemed? Would we ever risk disarmament and go the way of radical trust? Would we be spared a nuclear holocaust?

I could only ask the questions but the rainbow arching over the earth felt like a 'partial glimpse' of God's new creation. And in the meanwhile, as I listen to and hear even a fraction of what is happening in the whole cosmos, I have a choice as to whether I am going to live each day creatively or destructively, co-operating with the living creator God, or putting my own gods at the centre.

5

Listening to Paradox

We have explored a variety of approaches to listening to the world. Starting with our immediate environment we can learn to listen not only with our ears but also our eyes, heart, mind and conscience to what is going on around us. Gradually we become aware of issues arising from our context, to do with justice and injustice, poverty and wealth, work and unemployment, etc. We see how such issues affect people in ways we may need to question or challenge and respond to. As we do so we need constantly to be aligning ourselves to God's values of justice and righteousness and Kingdom living, so that we are learning to hear with his ears. We need also to listen within a biblical framework or world-view so that God's perspective becomes increasingly ours.

We will also soon become aware of our own attitudes to the world. Is my tendency to switch off from world affairs ('can't cope'), or to become activist ('better to keep working than stand still'), or to insulate myself in some form of individualism ('better to do my own thing')? As we listen to ourselves we gradually discover our vulnerabilities and defences – when we need to protect ourselves and when we need to be less self-protective and open ourselves more generously to the world in which we live. Sometimes we will need to become more involved in the outer world, at other times we will need to spend time on the inner world – our inner journey to maturity. The question is, what is being asked of me now by way of responsible involvement in the world of which I am a part?

Often our listening will confront us with seeming contradictions – realities which are equally true yet which feel uncomfort-

126

able, unnerving and which shake our longing for consistency. Five minutes ago I was looking at a sun-filled garden bright with daffodils, fresh green buds and singing birds and thinking, 'God's in heaven, all's right with the world'. Then I opened a letter with news of a bad rail accident involving Christian students crossing a railway line. *Is* God in his heaven since all is manifestly not right with the world? Yet both are realities – the beauty of the morning *and* the grim accident. If I follow my instinct for life and joy and shut my ears to the pain, I risk becoming triumphalistic. If I become mesmerised by the pain and suffering and block out the joy and hope, I risk becoming cynical or despairing. How can I listen to both, believing that 'he has the whole world in his hands'?

For me, part of the answer lies in being prepared to hear and live with the discomfort of paradox, which is not the same as contradiction or compromise but an acknowledging as true what feel like opposites – joy *and* pain, strength *and* weakness, hope *and* despair, life *and* death. Charles Elliott describes paradox as 'lived truth'. He says, 'Paradox is the least inadequate vehicle for catching that quality of truth, because it can both hold in tension two opposites and simultaneously point to a resolution of those opposites that includes them but transcends them.'[45]

Paradox can make for uncomfortable listening. Intellectually it leaves me helpless and longing for certainty – I felt it again recently when, over a joyful meal with three Czechoslovakian women, we celebrated their new-found freedom. We laughed, rejoiced, thanked God, wept tears of gratitude. *And* we looked at photographs of a bloodstained wall where students had been badly beaten, wreaths of flowers laid down in Wenceslas Square, and we talked of the ongoing bitter struggles of their neighbours in Romania. Joy and pain, hope and despair, life and death all in close and uneasy conjunction. No wonder Charles Elliott goes on to say, 'The mind will never apprehend the truth of paradox. Only the heart can do that'.[46] So how can we learn to listen from the heart?

Jean Vanier describes the experience like this:

Often our experience in life
is of being pulled between two poles:
the poles of ecstasy and pain,
the glory and the cross:
      our hearts are lifted up
      in the splendour of the cathedral
      with the sound of heavenly music,
      . . . the consciousness of centuries
      giving glory to the majesty of God.

Our hearts are stricken in pain
before the world of apparently meaningless
suffering,
hunger,
imprisonment,
death,
children killed in the womb
   . . . people dying without dignity.

 . . . Each of us is called to experience both
      ecstasy and pain
shunning neither one nor the other,
but entering into that mystery
where one leads to the other,
where misery and mercy embrace
and wholeness rises from brokenness.[47]

Not 'shunning' but 'entering into that mystery' where, opening ourselves to the seeming contradictions, we experience
them coming together in a reconciling 'embrace'. The centre
point of that reconciliation is Jesus. It is as we stand before
God, letting our mind descend into our heart, that we can best
listen to his world and discover that inner solidarity with others,
the fruit of which is compassion and the source of which is
Jesus, who has, by his dying for the world, reconciled all things
to God.

This struck me freshly one day when, walking through York
Minster, I saw a modern free-standing wood sculpture of the

Pieta. The figure of Christ lying on the ground was fashioned from a large tree trunk with separate pieces of wood lying there as twisted limbs, ugly nails protruding. Splits in the wood resembled deep gashes and wounds. Some parts of the body had been worked out in detail – the long, sensitive fingers of one hand lifted towards his mother, the feet and toes cut and vulnerable – whilst with others the bulk of the cracked wood spoke for itself. Nearby stood Mary, carved from another great tree trunk with the splits in the wood running down from the top of her head through her sad, tender face to where her robe touched the ground. Her gentle hands reached down towards her son. On both figures, in contrast to the cuts and gashes, strips of beaten brass were fixed to different parts of their bodies, patterned and glinting in the light. A graphic fusion of suffering and glory.

Fenwick Lawson, the sculptor, was inspired for his work by Michelangelo's *Rondanini Pieta* in Milan in which he saw the paradox of death and resurrection depicted. Of his own work he wrote,

> I have tried to embody the same duality of meaning; death is perceived through the brutalised, crucified body, the bruised, bent knees and the dismembered, unformed arm . . . Resurrection and life are expressed through the lifting arm and the dynamic of the hand hanging on to the mother . . . The polished brass as a metaphor for light is meant to reinforce this. The mother also offers a duality of meaning . . . the trauma of bereavement . . . and God's chosen vehicle for life giving. She . . . offers on the life through sacrificial death to the viewer.[48]

In our endeavours to listen to the world, we shall sometimes find ourselves drawn into the groanings and pain of the universe and at other times be given glimpses of the glorious freedom and fulness of life that is yet to come.

As we listen in Christ to the paradox we shall know in an ever-deepening way what Julian of Norwich was shown in her thirteenth revelation, that sin is a reality, 'but all shall be well, and all shall be well, and all manner of things shall be well'.

Exercises

Again, these may be used for personal reflection or sharing in a group.

Introduction
1. Go on a listening walk around your local area using your ears, eyes, heart, mind and conscience.
   — What is the atmosphere of the area? (e.g. friendly? impersonal?)
   — What sort of housing is there?
   — Is it a settled community or are people on the move?
   — Are people neighbourly and supportive or is there much loneliness?
   — Is there a cross-section of age groups?
   — What are the places and problems of work in the area?
   — Where are the places where people meet and share together?
   — Are there recreational facilities for the children? and adults?
   — What community needs are there that are not being met?
   — Is there anything you or your church could do about this?
   — As you think about your area, do you sense God is saying anything to you or your church?

Chapter 1   Listening to the Structures
1. What are some of the live current issues in your area? (e.g. housing, unemployment, minority groups, care of the elderly, etc.)
2. What are some of the issues raised for you by your work context? (e.g. working conditions, lack of fulfilment, difficult ethical questions, etc.) Or the street you live in? Or the shops you use?
3. In what ways is your church scratching where the local itches are?

4. Is God saying anything to you about these?[49]

Chapter 2   Listening to the Nation
1. As you watch, listen to or read the national news, is there
    any one particular area of injustice that stands out for you?
    What is particularly unjust about it? Is there anything you
    can or want to do about it?
    Look out in the national news for an example of where
    unrighteousness is being righted.
2. Find an example of where the Kingdom of God is not only
    being talked out but demonstrated by a church (e.g. church
    housing for the elderly, a Sharing Fund for the poor, pro-
    vision for the homeless, etc.).

Chapter 3   Listening to the World
1. How do you keep informed about world news?
2. Do you identify with any of the attitudes described on p.
    105? How would you describe your own attitude to world
    affairs?
3. Does the biblical framework of Creation, Fall, Redemp-
    tion, New Creation alter your perspective on world events?
    If so, how?
4. Take a news item and meditate on it, putting yourself in
    the scene and asking the Holy Spirit to guide you.

Chapter 4   Cosmic Listening
1. Is there a particular environmental issue that concerns you?
    How are you channelling your concern?
2. In what ways have you or your church been aware of/in-
    volved in spiritual warfare in your area? (e.g. ouija boards,
    occult practices, dark or oppressed places or buildings,
    etc.)

Chapter 5   Listening to Paradox
1. What for you are vulnerable or difficult topics of news
    where you need to protect yourself?
2. In what ways do you need to open yourself more gener-
    ously to the world?

3. What for you have been helpful symbols of death and
    resurrection?

References

1. David Sheppard and Derek Worlock, *Better Together* (Hodder & Stoughton, 1988), p. 196.
2. *ibid.*, p. 136.
3. *ibid.*, p. 149.
4. Jean Pierre de Caussade, *Self Abandonment to Divine Providence* (Fontana, 1971), p. 112.
5. Bruce D. Rumbold, *Helplessness and Hope: Pastoral Care in Terminal Illness* (SCM Press, 1986), p. 122.
6. John Stott, *Issues Facing Christians Today* (Marshalls, 1984), pp. 13,14.
7. Norman Snaith, *Distinctive Ideas of the Old Testament* (London, 1944), pp. 76ff, quoted by David Sheppard and Derek Worlock, *op. cit.*, p. 137.
8. John V. Taylor, *Kingdom Come* (SCM, 1989), p. 20.
9. Leslie C. Allen, *Micah's Social Concern, Vox Evangelica VIII* (ed. Donald Guthrie, London Bible College, 1973), p. 29.
10. A phrase used by John Goldingay in his inaugural lecture (as Principal of St John's College, Nottingham), 'The Bible in the City'.
11. C. J. H. Wright, *Living as the People of God* (Inter-Varsity Press, 1983), pp. 43–4.
12. *ibid.*, p. 44.
13. The Report of the Archbishops' Commission on Urban Priority Areas, 1985.
14. Michael Harper, *Let My People Grow* (Hodder & Stoughton, 1977), p. 51.
15. Charles Elliott, *Praying the Kingdom* (DLT, 1985), p. 11.
16. *ibid.*, p. 12.
17. A phrase used by Thomas Cullinan, *The Passion of Political Love* (Sheed & Ward, 1987), p. 107.
18. John Stott, *op. cit.*, p. 33.
19. *ibid.*, p. 34.
20. Christopher J. H. Wright, *The Use of the Bible in Social Ethics* (Grove Books, 1983), p. 7.

21. *ibid.*, p. 8.
22. *ibid.*, p. 8.
23. Richard Foster, *Celebration of Discipline* (Hodder & Stoughton, 1980), p. 28.
24. Ed. Naomi Tutu, *The Words of Desmond Tutu* (Spire, 1989), p. 37.
25. *ibid.*, p. 37.
26. Sheila Cassidy, *Sharing the Darkness* (DLT, 1988), p. 144.
27. Desmond Tutu, from an address at St Albans Abbey, 1988.
28. Shirley du Boulay, *Tutu, Voice of the Voiceless* (Penguin, 1989), p. 98.
29. Charles Elliott, *op. cit.*, p. 36.
30. Gerard W. Hughes sj, *God of Surprises* (DLT, 1985), p. 73.
31. Henri Nouwen, *Reaching Out* (Collins, 1976), p. 57.
32. Lawrence Osborn, *Meeting God in Creation* (Grove Books, 1990), p. 14.
33. Quoted by Ian Bradley, *God is Green* (DLT, 1990), p. 48.
34. Ian Bradley, *op. cit.*, p. 6.
35. *ibid.*, p. 39.
36. Barbara Wood, *Our World, God's World* (The Bible Reading Fellowship, 1986), p. 22.
37. News items from *The Daily Telegraph*, 8 March 1990.
38. Final Conference Statement from 'The Changing Atmosphere: implications for global security', Toronto 1988. Quoted in World Wild Fund for Nature Review (1988/89) p. 23.
39. Printed in *The Listener*, 9 March 1989, p. 7.
40. Quoted by Walter Wink, *Unmasking the Powers*, (Fortress Press, 1986), p. 141.
41. E. F. Schumacher, *The Economics of Conservation*, quoted by Barbara Wood, *Our World, God's World* (BRF, 1986), p. 49.
42. John R. W. Stott, *God's New Society* (IVP, 1979), p. 263.
43. Ian Bradley, *op. cit.*, p. 106.
44. John V. Taylor, *op. cit.*, p. 69.

45. Charles Elliott, *Praying through Paradox* (Fount, 1987), p. 19.
46. *ibid.*, p. 44.
47. Jean Vanier, *The Broken Body* (DLT, 1988), pp. 61,62.
48. Fenwick Lawson, printed commentary on display with wood sculpture, York Minster, April 1989.
49. See Fran Beckett, *Called to Action* (Fount, 1989) for a useful Community Survey Questionnaire.

Section 4

Listening to God

Introduction

Christians believe in a *God who speaks*. Ours is not a silent God, a God who sits, sphinx-like, looking out unblinking on a world in agony . . . He speaks *because he loves*. Love always seeks to communicate.

(Donald Coggan)[1]

Looking at the different sections of this book it may appear as if listening to God is a separate activity from listening to myself, others or the world – as though one is *either* listening to another person *or* to God, *either* listening to world news *or* to God. There clearly are times when we will hear God as we listen to ourselves, others, the world, for he is in all things. There are other times when, as Jesus did, we will need to stand back from our daily context to hear him more clearly. We shall look in more detail at these different stances later on in this section.

As we move into the 1990s we notice a phenomenon that may at first look contradictory. Increasing secularism has meant that God is no longer seen as being at the centre. The human person has taken that place. Lesslie Newbigin said,

> The way of understanding the world now has a quite different centre. We no longer teach our children that the central reality with which they will have to deal is God and his purpose. We no longer teach as a factual statement that the chief end of man is 'to glorify God and enjoy him forever' . . . The central reality of history is the human person, armed with modern science and technology.[2]

Yet there is also a felt need on the part of many (and not only Christians) to make sense of the inner life, to find a spirituality that satisfies. Amidst the intense materialism of this age there is also a search for meaning, for words that count. Some are drawn to the East, others turn to monasteries and convents (though not necessarily to the institutional Church).

Words spoken off the top of our heads are useless, ringing hollow to the recipient; words that count will come from the heart where they have been heard, reflected on, received as nourishment, digested and shared with others as food for the journey. And the good news is that the God who has always wanted to share his Word with us, still does. Just as he frequently said to Israel, 'Hear, O Israel', 'listen to me', 'give ear to me', and as Jesus was constantly listening to his Father so that he could say, 'I do nothing on my own but speak just what the Father has taught me', God's desire still is to speak to us. Our own desire to listen will depend, in part at least, on who we believe him to be.

No one particularly wants to relate to a God who is dictatorial, bossy and out to catch us. But then neither do we want one who is weak and ineffective. The truth is we can never with our finite minds grasp God for he is mystery. But mystery is not the same as unknowable or beyond experience. He has made himself known in Jesus and he invites us to experience him. Yet the image we have of him will greatly influence our desire to listen and respond to him. Gerard Hughes' identikit caricature of 'Good Old Uncle George' is not so far removed from how many people think of God.[3] For some, he is the celestial policeman and I'd better keep on the right side of him. For others he may be too weak even to challenge me, yet he needs my flattery and appeasement. Or he may be so distant and remote that there's little point in making an approach, except in times of dire need. At a workshop on Images of God, the variety offered by people was revealing – 'imaginary and irrelevant', 'killjoy', 'the chaser', 'the guilt maker', 'the keeper of the balance sheet'. One lady recalled, when she was seven years old, her R. E. teacher standing over her, red-faced and angry, shouting, 'You *will* believe that God loves you!' Inadequate images are far more widespread than we may think and can prove a serious block to our personal healing and growth. Gerard Hughes writes, 'the particular image we have of God will depend very much on the nature of our upbringing and how we have reacted to it, because our ideas and our felt knowledge derive from our experience'.[4]

My own childhood god was large with a long flowing white beard. He shouted, liked noise and clamour and had a distinct preference for Salvation Army bands. In fact he bore a strong resemblance to an imposing sepia photograph which hung over the fireplace in my grandparents' front room. It was a picture of William Booth, founder of the Salvation Army. I remember puzzling over how busy he always seemed to be, especially on Sundays when, if you wanted to stay in his good books, you went to as many meetings as possible. If I'd been less frightened of him I'd have asked him why he didn't approve of family time and fun together on Sundays. But I never dared. I was scared stiff of him. And, although I came by a different route to personal faith, it was years before I could face going to church without having panic attacks. Even on the warm, sunny day when, in my mid-thirties, I was confirmed into the Church of England, I was tearful and anxious. I can still sometimes catch myself out as I approach prayer with negative expectations of doom and gloom. Yet I am discovering that God's forgiveness is far more creative than my self-condemnation, his faithfulness more generous than my anxious fears. As the old image withers in the light of his reality and the distortions gradually give way to his truth, I am finding he really is the God of surprises and I am drawn to him.

Whatever our own particular images of God, we need, gradually or suddenly, to come to that place of experiencing him as our loving Creator who is *for* us. Before ever he demands a thing of us, he gives himself to us in love, mercy and healing. It is as we come to know who he really is that our desire to listen to, hear and respond to him will grow.

1

Listening in the Market Place

As the Gospel writers give us glimpses of Jesus at prayer, we see a pattern emerging of involvement and withdrawal. During the three years of his ministry we see him constantly surrounded by people – teaching, preaching, healing, confronting evil, training his disciples and initiating his Father's Kingdom. At the beginning of his Gospel Mark describes a day in the life of Jesus as he taught authoritatively in the synagogue at Capernaum, confronted and drove out evil from a man who was present, healed Peter's mother-in-law, healed a crowd of sick and demon-possessed people (Mark 1:21–34). This, for him, was the 'market place' with its constant exposure to the pressures and demands of needy men, women and children. Yet in the midst of it all, sometimes at night and sometimes in the early morning, he would suddenly withdraw to be alone. 'Very early in the morning, while it was still dark, Jesus got up, left the house and went off to a solitary place where he prayed' (Mark 1:35). Similarly, after the drama of feeding the 5,000, he dismissed his disciples and the lingering crowd and 'went into the hills to pray' (Mark 6:46). In order to maintain the momentum of Kingdom activity, he periodically went apart into the company of his Father where he could find fresh strength, perspective, belonging. This, for him, was the 'desert', sometimes a real one and sometimes a garden or hillside. There he would be with his Father in heart to heart communion, aligning himself freshly to his Kingdom plans. We have much to learn from this rhythm of involvement and withdrawal, listening to God in the midst of our daily life and work – our market place – and knowing when and how to withdraw to the desert, not to escape but to give undivided attention to God and hear him more clearly. 'Desert or market place, it is not a question of pitching our tent in one or the other, but of learning to go forth and withdraw as the needs of our brother and the needs of our spirit demand.'[5]

In this and the following chapter we shall think more about this rhythm and how we can experience it for ourselves for, 'If action is out of touch with an interior source in prayer it eventually becomes arid and barren, and we find ourselves the victims of busyness, frenetic over-activity. But conversely, if our prayer becomes cut off from action it is cut off from life. Here is the equilibrium of contemplation and action'.[6]

Jesus knew his Father to be present at all times and in all places – except for that God-forsaken moment on the cross when he bore the full weight of the world's sin. His Father had made the world and, as Jesus walked through it, he listened to and heard him in all things. He grew up surrounded by the sights and sounds of everyday life in Nazareth – Joseph's workshop, the smells, colours and bustle of the streets, the shops, stalls and animals. His parables are full of the things he noticed – a coin, a wineskin, mending, a lamp, sweeping, yeast and bread, wooden yokes and fishing nets. As he walked the dusty roads with his disciples he listened to and heard his surroundings – a fig tree, grass, a lily, sheep, birds, a mother hen and her chicks, the sky and the wind. One gets the impression of a man who, however busy, had time to look and listen, not just with a glance but in a receptive and contemplative way. 'Look at the birds of the air', 'see how the lilies of the field grow'. The verbs used indicate far more than a passing glance. 'Take a good look at', he says. 'Look and learn from them', 'hear their significance'.

> Contemplation is not, as people often mistakenly believe, chiefly a matter of advanced techniques in prayer, a secret knowledge of mysteries . . . It is primarily a way of looking and listening, of beholding, marvelling, considering.[7]

Jesus both modelled and taught a way of life that was not

world-transcending but world-affirming, a constant discovery
of the Father in all things. And this included the city as well
as the countryside. As he listened to Jerusalem, he wept and
grieved that its inhabitants were so deaf to their own needs.

How can we live in this contemplative way, seeing and hearing God in all things? The challenge came home vividly to me
one evening as I watched a party of Moslems get out of their
minibus in the crowded car park of Watford Gap service station
on the M1 motorway. Facing the setting sun they unrolled their
prayer mats and prostrated themselves in prayer. It jolted me
into realising that God was as present there as in the church
and countryside I had visited earlier that day.

Brother Lawrence, a seventeenth-century monk, discovered
how he could open himself to God amidst the ordinary tasks
of each day. He practised the presence of God by 'simple
attentiveness' in the monastery kitchen where he worked.
Whilst scrubbing the floor or cooking food he could say, 'He
talks with me and his ceaseless pleasure is my company in a
thousand thousand ways'.[8] His regular prayer was, for him,
'only a continuation of this practice'. He used visible things to
become more open to the invisible. We can do likewise, expecting God to come to us in and through what we see and hear
and touch in our daily lives. Esther de Waal writes, 'Seeking
God does not demand the unusual, the spectacular, the heroic.
It asks of me as wife, mother, housewife that I do the most
ordinary, often dreary and humdrum things that face me each
day, with a loving openness that will allow them to become
my own immediate way to God'.[9] Sometimes my own 'loving
openness' is no more than a bleary-eyed 'Yes' to God as I wake
in the morning, but that is enough to indicate my desire to be
open to him and hear him in a new day. Phyllida, at Ffald-y-
Brenin, finds that sometimes as she weeds and prunes in the
garden and washes up dirty crockery at the sink – jobs she
doesn't particularly enjoy – she can sense God reminding her
she is a co-worker in his ongoing work of redemption. The jobs
can take on a different quality when seen in that light.

When I remember, I pause before making or answering a

phone call or writing a letter, to open the act to God – he may want to speak to or through me in it. And, when some days seem full of interruptions, I recall the old professor at Notre Dame University who told Henri Nouwen, 'You know . . . my whole life I have been complaining that my work was constantly interrupted, until I discovered that my interruptions were my work'.[10] If interruptions to my well-laid plans are God's messengers, am I open to receive them? Our slowness to hear God is not that he is reluctant to speak but that we are reluctant to listen. Each night I recall the events of the day, asking God to show me when he came to me. Yesterday it was through a Bible verse, an encouraging phone call, practical help given by friends, an apple tree full of pink and white blossom, standing alongside a bereaved friend. 'Advent moments' when he comes freshly, unexpectedly, to surprise, delight, challenge and show us the way.

Not only was Jesus aware of his Father in all things but the Gospel accounts give the impression that, amidst the activity of each day, there was an ongoing dialogue between Father and Son. As the seventy-two disciples returned from their mission and joyfully shared with Jesus what had happened, he spontaneously said to his Father – 'I praise you, Father, Lord of heaven and earth, because you have hidden these things from the wise and learned, and revealed them to little children. Yes, Father, for this was your good pleasure' (Luke 10:21). Before raising Lazarus to life, he looked up and said, 'Father, I thank you that you have heard me. I knew that you always hear me, but I said this for the benefit of the people standing here' (John 11:41,42). In pastorally sensitive situations he spoke with amazing appropriateness – the kind of wisdom that often left his onlookers speechless. When an adulteress was dragged to him, in the highly charged atmosphere around him, Jesus was silent as he wrote on the ground. Was he listening to his Father? When he spoke, it was with a devastating simplicity that caused the crowd to melt away. 'If any of you is without sin, let him be the first to stone her' (John 8:7). He was silent again before welcoming the woman into new life and

hope with the God-given words, 'Neither do I condemn you.
Go now and leave your life of sin' (John 8:11). He was constantly speaking out of that wisdom, truth and love whose
source is God. The Servant Song in Isaiah 50 is a telling back-
cloth to the dénouement of Jesus' ministry as the Word of God:

> The Sovereign Lord has given me
>   an instructed tongue,
>   to know the word that sustains
>   the weary.
> He wakens me morning by morning,
>   wakens my ear to listen like
>   one being taught.
>   (Isaiah 50:4)

Not only was Jesus attuned to his Father's wisdom but also
to his timing. Some days there was an urgency to move on to
a different place (Mark 1:38), on others a deliberate delay
(John 11:6). In all the pressures of his ministry we never see him
flustered or at a loss – he moved forward with quiet purpose, as
though walking out a divine timetable. Whilst he was uniquely
the Son of God, what prevents us, as children of the same
Father, from listening as he did?

Many of us are more conditioned by a materialistic world-
view than we realise so, although at one level we believe God
speaks, we don't move into each day with a sense of expect-
ancy. Or perhaps we think compartmentally – God might speak
to us in church but not in the office or kitchen. Or maybe we
think that, if he is going to speak to anyone, it will be to
someone important rather than me. I once heard, in a radio
play, an old man telling a younger man who had said God
wanted to talk to him, 'Why should God want to talk to *you*?
If he wants to talk to someone he's got the Archbishop of
Canterbury and the Queen and the vicar and – well, people
like that, hasn't he?' The good news is that the Christian's God
is one who speaks, not just to the high and mighty but to all
his people. 'He speaks *because he loves*. Love always seeks to
communicate.'[11] And his communications are not reserved for

certain places or days of the week for 'the path of God leads through the very middle of my most daily routine'.[12]

Like Jesus, we can cultivate an inner dialogue with God in the midst of daily life, sometimes talking to him, sometimes listening, opening our concerns, questions, hopes, fears, turning to him with a love glance and feeling his loving response, asking for wisdom for others or for his perspective on a particular task. We do not have to go apart or kneel down before God will speak to us. He is with us continually whether we feel his presence or not.

Derek is part of a high-powered management group and often, as they meet to discuss business, he is quietly holding it all to God, listening for his perspective. On one occasion feelings were running high as they wrestled with what felt like an intractable problem. As Derek was asking God for light, 'I was suddenly given the complete scenario. It was quite outside of my own experience yet God gave insights which seemed to fit'. He shared these with the group and within fifteen minutes the situation was transformed.

'How did you think of it all?' asked one man afterwards.
'I was praying', Derek replied.
'That's some God you've got!' the man said, with a sense of awe.

Michael, when he was a doctor in General Practice, sometimes had thirty patients to see in a morning. 'Sometimes I felt a distinct kick from God, an inner feeling that I should offer to pray with a patient. I'd look at my watch and think, Help! I've only got seven minutes per person . . . how will I get through? Yet each time it happened, God honoured it. Either the next patient didn't turn up or just wanted a quick visit for a sick note.' This simple availability to God in the midst of daily work is not a guarantee for instant solutions but is a way of opening situations to him.

Once, during a consultation of pastoral counsellors, social workers, clergy and others, when discussion was becoming somewhat fragmented, Bishop Maddocks, who was chairman, said, 'Let us be quiet for a few moments and listen to God'. In the silence the confusion of words cleared and, on resuming the discussion, we saw the way forward again. A useful procedure for many a committee or P.C.C. meeting!

There is a way of ordering our mental life on more than one level at once. On one level we may be thinking, discussing, seeing, calculating, meeting all the demands of external affairs. But deep within, behind the scenes, at a profounder level, we may also be in prayer . . . and a gentle receptiveness to divine breathings.[13]

Listening to God in this way does not add to our work but rather is a means of opening every part of what we do to the One who is always waiting to share himself with us more fully.

Perhaps our greatest need in listening to God in the market place is for a still centre, an available space deep within ourselves where we can receive and respond to what he says. We see it clearly modelled in Jesus. Never flustered or caught off guard, he walked out each day in loving obedience to his Father. This was the centre point of his life, the heart of his whole ministry. 'I do nothing on my own but speak just what the Father has taught me' (John 8:28).

So often our inner space becomes cluttered and unavailable as we find ourselves driven by conflicting motives and forces. Yet God invites us to 'make a chapel of our heart, to which we can from time to time withdraw to have gentle, humble, loving communion with him'.[14] In the midst of each day's pressures we can move in and out of our inner chapel which will, with use, gradually become a safe place where we can reflect on and respond to what we hear in the market place. And, as we commune with Jesus there he, the Word of God, will gradually become the centre and heart of our living.

2

Listening in the Desert

Jesus was no superman who could move through the demands and pressures of each day without being affected. Because he was genuinely and fully human he became wearied by the pressure of constant crowds – their needs, wounds, words, arguments, intrigues and attacks. He needed solitude and regularly found it. Sometimes it was in the midst of demanding ministry (Mark 1:35), sometimes he wanted to be alone for uninterrupted prayer – for his disciples, his family, his friends and those he met in daily life. At other times he withdrew after significant acts of healing (Luke 5:16), or meeting human need (Mark 6:46), or in preparation for a major event in his ministry, such as his transfiguration (Luke 9:28) or crucifixion (Matthew 26:36). There was also the forty days in the arid Judean desert when, in solitude, he fasted, prayed and battled against the powers of darkness.

> There he was tempted with the three compulsions of the world: to be relevant . . . to be spectacular . . . and to be powerful . . . There he affirmed God as the only source of his identity . . . Solitude is the place of the great struggle and the great encounter – the struggle against the compulsions of the false self, and the encounter with the loving God who offers himself as the substance of the new self.[15]

It was here too in the desert that Jesus experienced what he would constantly be teaching others, that 'man does not live on bread alone, but on every word that comes from the mouth of God' (Matthew 4:4).

For all these reasons Jesus periodically withdrew, yet there

was a further one too. Intimate company with his Father was
Jesus' chief resource and succour. His home was in 'the bosom
of the Father' (John 1:18 AV), his mission was 'to do the will
of him who sent me' (John 6:38), his entire dependence was
on his Father for 'the Son can do nothing by himself' (John
5:19), his obedience to his Father was his nourishment, 'my
food is to do the will of him who sent me' (John 4:34). It was
in this close love relationship that Jesus most clearly knew
himself to be accepted and sustained. This was the place where
again and again his vision was renewed, his perspective
restored, his priorities re-aligned. His times of withdrawal were
not for selfish reasons but he refused to sacrifice the vital for
the pressing.

The example of Jesus challenges us to find a similar rhythm
of prayer through involvement and withdrawal – not either/or
but both/and. And the busier we are, the greater the challenge,
for the Gospel writers indicate that the effectiveness of his
ministry in the market place was strongly linked with his times
of withdrawal to the desert. 'Somewhere we know that without
listening speaking no longer heals, that without distance closeness cannot cure. Somewhere we know that without a lonely
place our actions quickly become empty gestures.'[16]

Withdrawal will never be easy and for some it will be impossible at certain stages of life, beyond the 'little solitudes'[17] found
in the midst of a working day. But as we see the point of it
and experience its value so we can know what to aim at.
'Intimacy with God does not develop without sacrifice',[18] wrote
a busy wife and mother as she looked back on planning her
first retreat. We might begin with part of a day and later
manage a whole day or weekend. We may begin at home
(though this is often unsatisfactory because of the many distractions there) or we may go to a friend's house or make for the
countryside or a retreat house or convent. It may take time
and experiment to find the best venue. We shall need to remind
ourselves that this kind of withdrawal is not escape or running
away from our daily life but a deeper engagement with it. Joyce
Huggett calls it 'withdrawal with a purpose'[19] – to meet with

God. And if we have doubts as to whether we can spare the time, we shall know its value later as the effects spill over into our everyday life and relationships.

There may be various circumstances that are nudging us forward into a time of extended quiet – a decision to be made, a sense of dryness or emptiness, heavy work commitments, or simply a longing to spend more time with God. How we use the time is a matter for personal choice and can be read about elsewhere.[20] It may be helpful to seek advice from someone more used to doing this and who knows us. Whatever our reason for withdrawing we are likely to discover four things – and probably many more. Firstly, silence, however much we long for it, is not always easy. It can be hard to stop both our bodies and our whirring minds. Distractions, thoughts, fantasies can abound or voices telling me this is a waste of time and there are far more useful things I could be doing. But if only I will quietly persist, not driving myself but taking time to quieten my body – perhaps by a slow awareness walk – and my mind – perhaps by focussing on the name of Jesus – other claims will begin to lose their urgency so that I gradually become still and open to God.

Secondly, solitude is indeed 'the place of the great struggle and the great encounter'. As I look to God so I see the false self that is still so much part of me and this can be unnerving. When I was caring for my mother in her terminal illness I used to go into the local church each lunch-hour for quiet prayer. Sometimes it felt like a port in a storm, at other times I was in turmoil. Our college term had begun, I had been given extended leave yet all I could think about was how I was missing out on the public and professional side of my life – the teaching and speaking engagements which gave me considerable satisfaction. A hidden ministry felt very second-best. As I sat alone in the church so I sensed God saying to me, 'Go the little way, the way of humility. Do not seek recognition but service. Do not strive for success but learn to stoop. Do not measure your efforts by how much people applaud you but by how much they see me in you.' It is so easy (for me at least) to take refuge in professionalism, yet here was God offering me the chance for ongoing conversion so that my identity depended less on what I did (works) and more on his loving action within me (grace). It is in solitude, in the presence of Jesus the Truth, that 'I get rid of my scaffolding' as Nouwen describes it, face up to my false self and take on a little more of the new self that God offers me in Christ.

Thirdly, it is in solitude that we can be met freshly by God's living Word. With a greater sense of leisure than is often possible in everyday life we can be more available to listen to God. Supremely that will be through Scripture which, God says, 'will not return to me empty but will accomplish what I desire' (Isaiah 55:11).

Karen went on an Ignatian directed retreat. 'As I read from the Bible (my only book) each day, the events of two thousand years ago became present to me and Jesus walked the hills with me. I reheard my call while exploring Peter's, in Luke 5. I experienced new birth as I became Nicodemus probing this issue with Jesus, in John 3. I was like a sheep following the voice of the shepherd as I walked through John 10. When I came to the Gethsemane passage the intensity was great. I whittled a walking stick out of a branch – a slightly different approach from the disciples. They fell asleep to escape. On the last day I climbed to the top of a hill and sang songs. Verses of Scripture came to me one after another. The experiences of that week are still with me. Now more than ever I am directing people to look at the Gospel incidents in order to gain strength through the objective truth of what our Lord did and said.'

Elizabeth, a busy wife, mother and doctor, carved out two days to go on her first retreat. After only twenty-four hours she was called away to her sick father and was with him when he died later that day. Yet God had already spoken to her as she read Psalm 62, 'He alone is my rock and my salvation'. Her retreat giver had also pointed out a verse describing Christ as the life-giving spiritual rock in the desert (1 Corinthians 10:3,4). She found this a deeply steadying and life-giving word over the next few days.

Because God's Word is alive and powerful it will search us out, comforting *and* challenging, reviving *and* rebuking, yet always in love. The silence of a retreat can give us the space and time to hear at greater depth. 'We will never be truly whole if we only know the need of a Saviour by hearsay', said a retreat leader. As I read the Gospel on that retreat I became uncomfortably aware of an area of failure I had not dared to look at before and where I only knew the need of a Saviour by hearsay, so it had remained buried and unhealed. As I fearfully asked God, '*Did* I fail?' I sensed he was saying, 'Yes and no. Yes, in that you backed away from what you would not face. No, in that I knew you wanted my will. I never left you during those dark days for it was out of your failure that I could bring your healing. Failure is not the end. It can be a fresh beginning.' I had never seen it like that before. Freshly forgiven, I wept for joy.

But God does not always speak to us in words. We may hear him through his created world, especially when we slow down, or through a picture or music. And sometimes, as we withdraw from people and noise we shall hear our own inner desire for him, a desire which is only a very pale reflection of his for us. He put it within us so that we might be drawn closer to him.

> You yourself are the place of desire and need. All your love, your stretching out, your hope, your thirst, God is creating in you so that he may fill you. It is not your desire that makes it happen, but his. He longs through your heart. Your insufficiency . . . is no barrier. In your prayer God is seeking you and himself creating the prayer; he is on the inside of the longing.[21]

Fourthly, something we shall realise often after rather than during a time of withdrawal, is that our involvement with and availability to others has grown. 'We cannot enter solitude, this great "God-alone-ness", and hold the world at arm's length. In solitude we are awakened more fully to people.'[22] Retreats are not primarily about self-awareness but God-centredness and becoming more available to him for his world. God wants to draw us close enough to himself to feel his heartbeat for our neighbours, our local community, our church, our nation, our world. If the consequences of a retreat do not bear evidence of this, there is something wrong. 'If human solidarity is forgotten, contemplation becomes no more than spiritual self-delusion.'[23] When we have been met freshly by God we have more to give to others, often in very practical ways, in our family or work context or community involvement. 'The more we receive in silent prayer, the more we can give in our active life.'[24]

So far we have been thinking of withdrawal in terms of the individual. But there is also a place for groups to listen to God together. Occasionally at St John's College if there was an important issue affecting us all, we would gather together in the chapel as a whole community for corporate silence in order to listen together to what God was saying. Then, with guidance from the Principal or Chaplain, we would share insights, Bible verses, pictures that had come to us in the silence. I have also sometimes helped churches do something similar at a parish Away Day or weekend. At one of these, when the church was at an important stage of needing to know the gifts of each person, they were encouraged as they met in groups of twelve to listen to God for each other. The anxiety that some felt as they began soon gave way to a deep sense of affirmation as each saw what he or she had to contribute. We need each other to discover and recognise the gifts God wants us to use for the upbuilding of his church.

Another example is from an Urban Priority Area church in a grey housing estate in the Midlands with a small group of people meeting together for an Advent course. Their ages ranged from twelve to eighty-one years, unemployed and a few employed and some of them newcomers – a vulnerable fellowship. The person leading them suggested one evening that they should have a kind of audience with God. She put a circle of night lights round the group and in the middle a large candle on a chair. She said, 'You can bring to God whatever questions you have and say what you like'. At first it was very quiet and the questions were hesitant, then they gathered force and speed. The stillness grew and the walls of the room seemed to drop away and the questions moved into the depths of prayer. 'Will there ever be peace and harmony?' someone asked. 'Why are people born handicapped?' 'Why don't you give us a few dramatic signs of your power, like striking bad 'uns dead?' 'What's going to happen to the empty flats at the top?' 'Is anyone listening?' 'Why do the most beautiful roses grow here?' 'Why did you take away the two people in my life that I really loved and trusted?' An old man suddenly called out, 'Who are you?' People said things they'd never dreamt of saying in front of each other before. And, as they listened, into the desolation came a sense of healing and arms encircling them. Someone spoke about the cross and Jesus' sufferings and the Gospel really began to grasp people. It was, said the vicar, something very special.

But for some people, the chance to withdraw or go on retreat is virtually impossible. The mother with young children, the father trying to build up his own business, the shift worker, will have very little freedom of choice over their use of time. Richard Foster writes about taking advantage of the 'little solitudes' that occur in our working day – before the family wakes up, sitting in a traffic queue, the few moments' breathing space between jobs. However busy, we can, even for a moment or two, learn to 'fashion our own desert . . . and dwell in the gentle healing presence of our Lord'.[25] Elizabeth, the doctor, sometimes does so for a few minutes in a lay-by as she drives to the clinic where she works. Alison does so as she walks the dog each morning, asking God to show her how to pray for her friends. Often as she listens a Bible verse comes to mind and she turns it into prayer for others. A Christian firm of architects begins each Monday morning by praying and listening to God for their working week and once a year the two senior partners review all that has happened, seeking God's perspective on their work.

Learning to find our desert places where we can, from time to time, withdraw to listen to God is complementary to finding and hearing him in the market place of our daily lives. This was the rhythm of Jesus and one that can become our own. Thomas Merton wrote,

> Action is the stream, and contemplation is the spring . . . It is for us to take care that these living waters well up in our own hearts. God will make it his own concern to guide our action, if we live in him, and he will turn the stream into whatever channels he wills . . . When action and contemplation dwell together, filling our whole life because we are moved in all things by the Spirit of God, then we are spiritually mature.[26]

3

Discerning God's Voice

Margaret had a hunch that she should visit Joy. Normally she would phone first but that day she simply arrived on the doorstep only to discover that Joy's mother had died the day before and that the surprise visit was both welcome and needed. Was Margaret's hunch from God or not? Martin was thinking about a job change. He came to talk about it and ask advice. Did he hear God through our discussion and his subsequent move, or not? Rob, a church member, had cancer. Some of the church felt God had clearly told them to pray for his cure and that he would not die. But he did and there is still pain and confusion in the church. What had gone wrong? So far we have considered different contexts for listening to God but how can we tell if we are actually hearing him? Are there reliable criteria for discerning his voice?

One definition of discernment is 'the capacity to perceive and interpret the religious and moral significance of experience in order to make an appropriate response to God'.[27] Another says, 'discernment has to do with identifying communications that come from God'.[28] Biblically it has different and inter-related shades of meaning. Firstly, it is about that wisdom whose origin is heavenly rather than earthly (James 3:13–17) and which comes from being in a right relationship with God. Secondly, it is something that all Christians are, at least in measure, to seek after and practise. 'Test all things', Paul wrote (1 Thessalonians 5:21). A particular example of such testing is seen in 1 John where believers are told to test those who claim to be prophets by discerning whether they are inspired by 'the Spirit of God' or by 'the spirit of the antichrist' (1 John 4:1–3).

The crux of the test is whether or not Jesus is recognised as the incarnate Son of God. Discernment 'begins in Christianity with a response of faith or of unbelief to Jesus himself'[29] in his incarnation and his lordship. Thirdly, in listing some of the spiritual gifts given by God for the upbuilding of the Church, Paul includes 'the ability to distinguish between spirits' (1 Corinthians 12:10), that is 'being able to separate spiritual manifestations at the point of their origins . . . The person who discerns has a special capacity to weigh things up and draw all the right conclusions from them.'[30] The origin of such spiritual manifestations may be divine or human or demonic. For example, when Jesus asked his disciples who he was, Peter answered with God-given discernment, 'You are the Christ, the Son of the living God' (Matthew 16:16). Shortly after, when Jesus predicted his death, Peter rebuked him, protesting that this would never happen. Jesus responded sharply, 'Out of my sight, Satan! . . . you do not have in mind the things of God, but the things of men' (Matthew 16:23). Whatever his motive, the origin of Peter's words was demonic. Later, after the death and resurrection of Jesus, when the Church was growing and Christians were sharing their possessions and money, Peter discerned that Ananias and Sapphira were secretly holding back part of their offering for themselves, thus lying to the Holy Spirit.

The use of discernment is wide-ranging, including personal choices made in everyday life, major life decisions, recognising and responding to God's communications both in the church and the world, teaching and counselling others. Another aspect worth noting, since many are experiencing it in retreats these days, is the Ignatian understanding of discernment involving prayerful self-reflection.

Discernment of spirits in everyday life involves us in a process of sifting our daily experience by noting and reflecting regularly on our affective responses to God and to life and its events . . . events in which we experience joy or sorrow, peace or turmoil, attractions or revulsions, an opening out to others or a narrowing in on ourselves, a sense of God's presence or absence, creativity or destructiveness.[31]

The purpose of reflecting in this way is that it not only deepens our self-understanding but also enables us to see more clearly where God is at work in our everyday life.

Discernment, then, is about sifting, separating out, identifying, interpreting, weighing, noting differences. And, at the heart of it, there is the gift and ability of recognising which, amongst other voices, is the voice of God.

John Powell wrote that there is always something 'surprising, distinctive and lasting about the communication of God'.[32] The surprise may be that he can speak when we are least expecting it and with a ring of truth that resonates within us. This was so for Abraham, Sarah, Jeremiah, Paul and it can be the same for us today. He will not speak to order, for he is not a push-button God. But we can cultivate the desire to hear him. The surprise may be that we are shown something from a fresh perspective. As I was pondering whether or not to accept the job I am now doing, I sensed God was asking me, 'Can you do this job?' Since it included a pioneering element and I didn't see myself as a pioneer, I heard myself responding with feeling 'No, Lord!' Then I sensed him saying, 'Can *I* do this job?' There seemed to me no doubt about that. 'Yes, Lord.' Then I sensed him quietly ask, 'So will you join me?' The penny dropped – it wouldn't be ME walking into the unknown but US! He would take the initiatives and I would follow him. In my usual slowness I hadn't seen it like that before.

God's communications are also distinctive. His voice has his characteristics – love, truth, peace, righteousness, justice, faithfulness, wisdom (James 3:17). When we sense we are hearing him, we can ask, 'Is it *like* God?' And, again, we shall get some surprises. Hearing him will not always be a comforting experience. Love is not the same as blandness and sometimes out of faithfulness his words will expose and judge us. It was the false prophets of Israel with their smooth promises of

'Peace, peace. No harm will come to you', whom God denounced through Jeremiah:

> I did not send these prophets,
>   yet they have run with their message;
> I did not speak to them,
>   yet they have prophesied. (Jeremiah 23:21)

To recognise God's voice we need to know him, his character and his ways, and spend time in his company. First and foremost this means immersing ourselves in Scripture.

> There are times when we hear and know that the inner voice which speaks is that of the Father, but we are only disposed to recognise his voice on those occasions *because* we have been trained to hear it daily in his word.[33]

It is the person whose 'delight is in the law of the Lord' and who 'meditates day and night' on it who will be blessed (Psalm 1:2). It is by constant feeding upon Scripture that we become mature, training ourselves 'to distinguish good from evil' (Hebrews 5:14). 'Without Scripture there is no discernment. Whatever wisdom we may have known, we swiftly lose if it is not sustained by Bible truth.'[34] It is as we stay close to God, reading and meditating on his word, letting it soak into every fibre of our being, that we get to know his character and his ways.

'Discernment is the fruit of a long "living with" the Lord'.[35] The supreme example of this is Jesus. For him, looking and listening to his Father were at the very heart of his ministry, 'the Son can do nothing by himself; he can do only what he sees his Father doing, . . . the Father loves the Son and shows him all he does' (John 5:19,20). Scripture is our touchstone for discernment and nothing we hear from God can ever contradict it. The so-called prosperity gospel of health, wealth and happiness is an example of the distortion that can happen in a materialistic age when those who claim to live by biblical truth miss out its teaching about justice, righteousness and mission.

Another characteristic of God's voice is that it brings clarity not confusion. I may feel confused about the issue I bring to

God, especially as his Spirit begins to move in me, searching me out and questioning me. I may also feel confused when life experiences challenge what I believe (as happened with some of Rob's church when he died). We should not try to avoid the feelings of confusion by stoically maintaining an unruffled tranquillity or phoney piety. God wants to make us more not less human. 'Turbulence . . . is not a sign that a person's feelings are not being touched by God. Rather, it may well be a sign that he is facing the realities of his situation.'[36] We shall find either that God gradually brings clarity into the confusion by what he says or that he is speaking his word into a level that is even deeper than the confusion and that somehow undergirds it. I found this happening frequently in the weeks preceding my mother's death. At one level I was experiencing turmoil and confusion. At another deeper level the Word and words of God were an undergirding reality.

Another characteristic of God's voice is its lasting quality. His words are not transient, but enduring and fruitful. His truth 'endures to all generations' (Psalm 100:5). His word does not return to him empty but 'will achieve the purpose for which I sent it' (Isaiah 55:11). So it will bear testing. And part of the process of discernment is to test out what we hear. Sometimes this will be by waiting rather than speaking or acting impulsively. Sometimes it will mean asking God for confirmation from Scripture or through circumstances, or through people who know us and whose insight we respect. And if we need encouragement for the times we mishear, we can remember Paul who 'tried to enter Bithynia, but the Spirit of Jesus would not allow them to' (Acts 16:7). Like him, we can be open to redirection and fresh advance.

Discernment also involves a growing understanding of ourselves and our own inner voices. This is not an invitation to endless introspection but rather to an honest knowledge of who we are. The alternative can be self-delusion, which Thomas Green describes as 'the unwillingness to know and face our real situation before the Lord.'[37] He likens it to a weed that can kill a whole harvest. I may weep out of sorrow for my sins *or* out of self-pity. I may be angry at someone behaving in a certain way because he is unscrupulous *or* because he is frail. We need to understand the differences. In Section One I have tried to look in more detail at what it means to listen to ourselves. It is an important part of the process of discernment. Is my basic orientation towards God and his Kingdom or myself and my own kingdom? Am I feeling happy because of God's goodness to me or because I am the centre of attention? It is as we get to know ourselves that we grow in discernment and as we grow in discernment so we get to know ourselves.[38]

It is not only for our own sake that we need self-understanding but also for others. If I feel I have been given an affirming word from God for someone else, it may be genuine or it may be nothing more than a projection of my own need to give comfort (though this need may be subconscious rather than known to me). If it were a critical word, again it may be genuine or it may be a projection of my own veiled criticism of that person.

> There is a fatal instinct in all of us to reduce the Word of God to the words of men, . . . There is the tendency to confuse our own dreaming and fancies with that listening that comes from the Spirit . . . This kind of listening is not always easy. It has little fiction, but much hope; little sentiment, but much love; little that is flattering, but much that is fulfilling.[39]

We will not always get it right, so will need to offer what we think God is saying in such a way that the other person will recognise whether or not it fits. John Gunstone, writing out of considerable experience of charismatic groups, says,

> there are occasions at prayer meetings or in counselling sessions when I have an inner conviction that something is not what it purports to be. It does not happen very often, but there is no mistaking this inner conviction . . . A prophecy may have been given which does not seem to call forth from me any response that I could believe was of the Spirit; . . . a

suggestion may have been made (perhaps prefaced by the words, 'the Lord tells me . . . ') which leaves me feeling uneasy.[40]

He helpfully points to how the Church has discerned true charismata from counterfeit through the centuries using as norms the authority of Scripture, the teaching of the Church, confirmation of the word given by other means and the results of spiritual gifts always being 'purifying, loving, edifying, uniting and strengthening. Above all, they glorify God, Father, Son and Holy Spirit.'[41] It is significant that five out of the nine gifts Paul lists in 1 Corinthians 12 are to do with listening to God – wisdom, knowledge, prophecy, discernment and the interpretation of tongues.

As we begin to discern the voice of God and our own inner voices, so we shall also learn to identify the presence of Satan, for he is not voiceless. When God is at work we can be sure that Satan is also. Though defeated, he is still alive and out to deceive us. We have clear indications from the names given to him in Scripture as to how he speaks. He is a tempter causing us to question God (Genesis 3:4,5). He leads people into bondage, crippling them physically, spiritually or emotionally (Luke 13:16). He is a liar who distorts the truth (John 8:44) and blinds people's minds so that they cannot see straight (2 Corinthians 4:4). He can masquerade as an angel of light (2 Corinthians 11:14). He can perform counterfeit signs and wonders (2 Thessalonians 2:9). He is a destroyer, prowling around like a roaring lion (1 Peter 5:8). He is an accuser who undermines believers (Revelation 12:10). These descriptions give us a clear idea of the range of his activities and deceptions. And it is as we experience and understand his ploys that we can grow in discernment. This will also be linked with self-understanding for if we know our own vulnerabilities we shall also know where we need God's protection. If we constantly find ourselves being tempted into negativity and fallacious thinking, or greed and consumer spending, or lust and riotous imaginings, especially where there is an element of compulsion, then we need to counter Satan's voice with God's truth and arm ourselves with the protection of Christ. The name of Jesus is powerful over every strategy of the Evil One and, as we learn to discern his presence and voice, so we can use our authority as children of God to remind him of Christ's victory, to rebuke, bind and dismiss him. 'Resist the devil and he will flee from you' (James 4:7).

'Discernment is at the heart of discipleship.'[42] If this is so then we must give it a high priority in our personal and corporate living. Here are some ways in which we can grow in discernment, not to be seen as rules but pointers. We can:

1. Ask God at the beginning of the day for a right orientation towards him and his Kingdom rather than me and mine. 'Lord, let my whole being be directed to your praise and service.'
2. Keep God's Word in our heart as our daily reference point.
3. Be open to God speaking to us at any time, through all aspects of our daily lives and especially through his created world.
4. Create inner space so that, however busy outside, we can, even momentarily, enter our 'inner chapel' to listen to God.
5. Practise 'little discernments' over how we spend our time or our money, how we choose which TV programmes to watch or which books to read.
6. Exercise discernment as we watch or listen to the news. What is God saying about national or international affairs? Where and how is Satan making inroads into nations and cultures and what is our responsibility in this?
7. Encourage our powers of observation and attention as we mix with people, enter a building, answer the phone. Being perceptive is part of discernment.
8. Turn to others whose insight we respect so that together we can discern what is happening and what God is saying.
9. Listen to God at the end of the day as we briefly review

it, thanking him for those moments or events, however small, where we were aware of him, and asking him to show us, through our feelings and attitudes, where we refused him entry.

10. Establish safe 'practice grounds' where we can learn to discern with and for each other, for example:

— in decision making. Peter was offered voluntary redundancy. He asked a group of eight friends to sit down with him, consider the facts and listen both to him and to God to discern the way forward. (It is more difficult for a group to be deceived than for an individual.)

— church leaders might set aside a day or half day to discern what God is saying about the way forward for the church.

— church groups or committees could make the habit of pausing briefly in the midst of business to listen to God together.

— those leading worship might include a short time in a service for corporate listening to God.

— house groups could include times of listening to God with and for each other, the sick, missionaries, local affairs, etc.

It is as we grow in discernment, learning to recognise God's voice, that the fruit of the Spirit becomes evident in our lives for 'far from producing a company of carping Christians eager to expose each other's faults, it develops the grace of merciful love among the people of God.'[43]

4

Listening and Responding

'Listening to God is one thing, seeing the situation with the eyes of Christ and responding is another', wrote a friend to me, a reminder that the kind of listening prayer we have been exploring is never an end in itself. God speaks to us so that we can respond in obedience. 'Prayer for me means becoming twenty-four hours a day at one with the will of Jesus to live for him, through him and with him',[44] said Mother Teresa – which sounds very much like James when he wrote, 'faith by itself, if it is not accompanied by action, is dead' (James 2:17). It would be strange if, out of the current desire that many are experiencing to learn about listening to God, there were not some significant advances in the ministry of the Kingdom. 'It is not enough to interpret the world. Our business is to change it. . . . Jesus spoke of *doing* the truth'.[45]

There are many examples in Scripture of men and women hearing God and responding in obedient action. Isaiah, worshipping in the temple, heard God asking, 'Whom shall I send? And who will go for us?' He responded, 'Here am I. Send me!' (Isaiah 6:8) Hearing led to obedience. Ananias, in Damascus, heard God calling to him in a vision. As he responded, he was told to go to a certain house, ask for Saul of Tarsus and heal his blindness. Not surprisingly, he hesitated, for Saul's reputation had gone before him. Yet, after further explanation, he went. Listening led to hearing and hearing to obedience (Acts 9:10–19). In Nazareth, the angel Gabriel appeared to Mary to tell her of God's plan for her to conceive and give birth to Jesus. 'How will this be, since I am a virgin?' As the plan was unfolded so she responded, 'I am the Lord's servant. May it be to me as you have said' (Luke 1:38). Again, listening led to a response of obedience.

The supreme example is in Jesus whose whole life was a daily response of loving obedience to his Father. We have noted already that what motivated his ministry was the burning desire to give expression to his Father's will. 'I have come down from heaven not to do my will but to do the will of him who sent me' (John 6:38). He who was God became human, humbled himself and 'walked the path of obedience all the way to death' (Philippians 2:8 TEV). The word 'obedience' is derived from the Latin *audire*, to hear. To obey is to hear then act upon what we have heard. 'We are not being truly attentive unless we are prepared to act on what we hear. If we hear and do nothing more about it, then the sounds have simply fallen on our ears and it is not apparent that we have actually heard them at all.'[46] By contrast, Jesus constantly listened, heard and responded to his Father. When he was twelve (the year of attaining Jewish adulthood), after Mary and Joseph had left Jerusalem to return home, Jesus stayed behind in the temple with the rabbis. He knew that his first obedience was to God and that he must be about his Father's business (Luke 2:49). 'The maturing centre of his life had been discovered and revealed. The boy who belonged to Mary had begun to be the man who belongs to God.'[47] It was from this intimate relationship of trustful obedience that all his ministry flowed. Even at the end as he agonised in Gethsemane over all that would happen, he could still say, 'Your will be done' (Matthew 26:42). And, even as he died, his last words were of personal commitment into the hands of Abba whose love he had proved all along and to whom he could respond in his dying also. 'Father, into your hands I commit my spirit' (Luke 23:46). 'This is not legal obedience driven by commandment, but trusting response to known love.'[48]

The word 'obedience' can evoke feelings of someone over and above, giving orders, imposing his will on me, a fearful, servile underling. I can still clearly recall with discomfort the panic I frequently felt in case I somehow misheard God's direc-

tion and ruined his plan for my life. Even when I sensed I was
hearing him there was still the likelihood that it wasn't him at
all but my imagination – a no-win situation full of red tape and
legalism. Fear conspires against obedience to the God 'whose
service is perfect freedom'. I was greatly helped by two pictures
from a Benedictine discussion of obedience.

> The Christian and monastic model for discerning God's will
> in a given situation is not that of finding the solution of a
> crossword puzzle where the answer must be exactly right,
> fitted to some preconceived plan. A better model is that we
> are given building blocks and have to see what can be done
> with them, using in the task all our intelligence, sensitivity
> and love.[49]

For me this insight into obedience helps to remove the neurotic
fear that 'I'll never get it right' and calls forth a more adult
response to a loving Father rather than a demanding task-
master.

Yet true obedience also leaves me in no doubt as to the One
I am to obey. It is possible to serve without obedience – WE
initiate, WE decide, WE are in control. WE may be doing
good *and* missing the point. Perhaps our service is motivated
more by fear than by love, perhaps we are driven more by our
own need for self-fulfilment than by loving response to what
the Father is telling us. Service that does not issue from trustful
listening to him may look useful but may also prove barren
and fruitless. Jesus taught, 'No branch can bear fruit by itself;
it must remain in the vine. Neither can you bear fruit unless
you remain in me' (John 15:4). He invites us to discover and
live out that creative consent which he himself experienced
with his Father – 'trusting obedience to known love'.

If listening to God is for obedient action then we need to be
open to the opportunities on our own doorstep. 'Prayer that is
unconcerned with the situation of our neighbour is pure self-
indulgence.'[50] Linda had advanced multiple sclerosis. She
couldn't get out of her wheelchair unaided nor could she feed
herself. She asked her doctor if he could find someone to visit

her 'who doesn't mind if I cry'. There were times when, because of the strength of her feelings, her facial muscles went into spasm and contorted her face. Her doctor asked Barbara, a widow, if she could go along and visit her. She did so and continued once a week for a year before Linda died, listening to her struggle with growing restriction and immobility. Linda's husband described Barbara as 'the lady who's brought joy into all our lives'.

Claire walks her dog each morning and, as she does so, prays and listens to God. She was feeling particularly concerned about Ruth, who sometimes came into the church coffee shop after working her night shift. Ruth and her husband had both spent their childhood in institutions and now they and their four children were being scapegoated by some of the locals and unjustly accused of vandalism, child abuse and incest. Ruth had poured it all out to Claire, including how they were going to be evicted and the children put into care. 'As I walked with the dog, a verse from Romans came to mind about God bringing what is dead to life and calling something out of nothing (Romans 4:17). I felt he was asking me to get involved. I'm no evangelist but I know I've been gifted to bring love and care to people and listen to them'. She offered to listen to the whole family as they shared their fears and frustrations with each other and started going to their home – only the second person they had ever allowed across their doorstep. She would sit in a deck chair whilst the children and parents sat on the bed and, as they talked, she would help them to hear each other and the hurts behind the words. Gradually social workers and Council house agents who needed to see them began to ask Claire to be present to help the family hear and understand what they were trying to say. She has also just offered to be present when their case is brought to court, to enable them to hear and understand, through all the official red tape, what is going on.

Ian and Pam have recently retired. He was a busy doctor in General Practice and she was a teacher. They belong to a cathedral congregation in the North of England. A few years

ago they were uncertain as to what the future held for them –
it felt like an 'expectant space', said Ian. Slowly the realisation
grew that they were being called to set up a service of listening,
available to other members of the congregation and later to
hurting people in the city. At the same time the Provost was
looking for a new use for a redundant entrance porch to the
cathedral. This was adapted, carpeted and furnished, changing
it into a comfortable room to which anyone can come who
needs listening to. In a variety of ways Ian and Pam felt God
was preparing them for a fresh chapter of service. Together
with the Provost they will be training a team of listeners who,
in the heart of a multi-racial city, will be there to listen to
people and to God for the needs around them.

Listening is only one of many ministries God might call us
to. It is not the particular ministry but our availability and
readiness to respond which matter. Much of what we are called
to will be humble, unacclaimed acts of service, a simple
response to what God was bringing to our attention. We may
be amazed when one day we hear Christ say to us, 'whatever
you did for one of the least of these brothers of mine, you did
for me' (Matthew 25:40).

> It is not the place where you are that is the important thing.
> It is the intensity of your presence there. It is not the situation
> that counts . . . [but] that you are fully alive in any situation.
> It is this that puts down roots and then flowers in your life.
> Availability: that is obedience. That and looking hard at the
> place where you are, instead of wanting to work wonders
> somewhere else.[51]

The Aston Cottage Community is the first of what is hoped
will be a number of small communities stemming from the Lee
Abbey Fellowship. In December 1988 two of them moved from
Devon to make their home in a small terraced house in Aston,
an Urban Priority Area in Birmingham, in partnership with
Aston and Handsworth Christians and the local parish church.
Now they are three, a Christian household living and worship-
ping together. They share a simple rule of life based on commit-

ment to Christ and to one another and, alongside the local churches, they seek to serve and be a sign of the Kingdom in a predominantly Muslim area. Next door is a home for mentally handicapped people and most of their neighbours in the street are Pakistanis, Bangladeshis and Afro-Caribbeans. About fifty per cent of households live in overcrowded conditions and unemployment is a major problem.

Each morning the Community read the Bible together and reflect on what the Word has to say about their daily life. Audrey said, 'Being here is about listening to God as we try to listen to the area and each other. We are learning about spiritual warfare, pain within families, tensions in the street and how to live together. Dave works as an assistant at a school for children with special needs and is also their escort as the school bus goes round picking them up each morning. He is on the committee of the local Residents' Association and has a growing friendship with the President of the nearby mosque. In their street lives a Muslim 'holy man' who resisted all attempts to talk with passers-by in the street. Dave prayed for an opportunity to get to know him and the answer turned up in the shape of the holy man's car outside the Community house with a flat tyre! Dave repaired it and the holy man started talking. Later he made Dave an offering of curry in a silver foil container, 'because you are a good neighbour!'

Audrey, after the death of a Muslim lady who lived in their street, felt God urging her to ask if she could go and sit with the women as they mourned. 'I couldn't get in for all the shoes in the hall. I took mine off and went into the front room which was cleared of furniture and had a white sheet on the floor. All the Muslim women in the street had come. I sat in a corner by the door – I didn't want to offend them. The two principal mourners sat opposite each other and rocked backwards and forwards wailing and all the others joined in. I felt I had to keep quiet, be with them and learn. I sat with my hands open and prayed silently in tongues. It was a case of sitting where they sat. The pain of misunderstanding between cultures so often blocks our hearing of them.' Audrey now visits two of them regularly to teach them English.

'The Kingdom in Jesus' teaching and action is not an interior spiritual matter only. It is set to transform the face of the earth and of human history.'[52] And it is a principle of the Kingdom of God that its workings often begin in small and hidden ways (Matthew 13:33).

This would be true for Christ Church, the Liverpool church described in the last section. When Clarry and Sue first went to Netherley, as they listened to the area they heard the frustration and despair of a community that had largely lost hope. Yet as they listened to God, they believed that he had a plan and purpose for Netherley and that he had placed within the community and church the resources to implement that plan. The church (at that time nineteen women and one man) needed to discover that they were 'an indispensable and integral part of all that God would do in Netherley, and that he wanted to use each one of them to fulfil his purposes. Each one was uniquely important.' This was the perspective that led them to develop a programme of lay training and leadership in the belief that 'the laity are not there to help the minister run the church. The minister is there to help the church change the world.'[53]

Many, including other clergy, said, 'there is no leadership material down there'. They were mistaken. Soon after their arrival Clarry and Sue started a Wednesday evening Bible study in their home which was, for many, their first experience of applying the Bible to their own lives. Gradually trust grew so that it also became a counselling and support group. Once a year Clarry and his curate took time to think about each church member and the new teaching or service he or she could embark on. Opportunities for meeting were made so that non-churchgoers could mix with church members – a playgroup for children so that their mothers could try out an informal Bible study, a weekly clothes cupboard, a community centre. Priority was given to worship, fellowship and mission. Gradually people were asked to help in worship – administering the bread and

wine, leading the prayers, giving out notices, occasionally leading and preaching. They learnt, during worship, to keep short
silences for listening to God, followed sometimes by spon-
taneous singing, praise, a tongue or prophecy. Prayer partner-
ships were developed, growth in sharing, trust, support. A
sense of mission to the local community also developed.

We have confronted Local Authority housing and Government policies. We have tried to make a contribution in the
debate about the need for resources to Inner Cities and the
Outer Areas, about Government employment, and benefits
policies . . . Above all, as we have looked at the area and
tried to see with the eyes of Christ, we have asked, 'what
are the needs of this area?'[54]

Early in his time there, Clarry became aware of his need for
a reference group of church members whom he could consult
more frequently than the monthly Church Council allowed for.
Gradually a group of ten became formalised as the Standing
Committee and met weekly to review Sunday services, the
minister's work of the past week, finance, the community
centre, any problems that had arisen. Each year the new
Church Council spent a day or more on retreat listening to
God for his priorities for the church in the next year. Of course,
this sort of lay training did not preclude mistakes yet it also
made for exciting growth and advance. 'For some it is their
first taste of community, or being of real value, or of being
treated with integrity and respect. For others there comes a
sense of God being the author of this chapter in their lives.'[55]

Kingdom living is about listening to God to hear what he is
doing and wants to do to bring in his Kingdom on earth.
'But how can what we are struggling to do possibly make any
difference?' some might ask. Yet

it is precisely by attempting the outrageous effrontery of
acting under God's control in a society that is not yet submit-
ted to it that the faithful make new discoveries about him
and learn to know him . . . And, because such obedience is

contrary to the way of the world, this way of the Kingdom needs to be embarked upon in company with other adventurers, learning with one another.[56]

5

A Listening God

So far we have been thinking about the different contexts and ways in which we can listen to, hear, recognise and respond to God's voice. For he is the God who speaks – in the market place and in the desert, through Scripture and through his created world, through people and through his still, small voice within us. But he is also a God who listens, who is 'always more ready to hear than we to pray'.[57] Listening is at the heart of God for he is not one but three, a Trinity of Father, Son and Spirit. Rublev's fifteenth-century icon of the Trinity depicts three angels looking at each other in mutual listening, loving and self-giving, three yet one in unity and purpose. It reminds us of the ceaseless communication that is going on within the Godhead.

In Scripture we see God constantly listening to his people. When they were oppressed in Egypt he heard their cry for help and their groaning (Exodus 2). When David was distressed, God heard him. 'He stooped to me and heard my cry for help' (Psalm 40:1, JB). When Jeremiah reached breaking-point and tried to repudiate his calling as a prophet, God heard him (Jeremiah 15). Jesus was constantly aware of his Father listening to him. 'Father, I thank you that you have heard me. I know that you always hear me' (John 11:41,42). And God does not simply listen like some inscrutable sphinx. He also takes action, reaching out in loving response to what he hears. He does this not by some remote control action but by drawing us into his purposes. As we listen to him we are sometimes given glimpses of what he is doing in response to the very need he has heard. He involves us in his acts of redemption.

So he not only heard the Israelites but caught Moses' attention by the burning bush, called him by name, shared with him his rescue plans for his people and appointed him to bring them out of Egypt (Exodus 3). God saw David's adultery with Bathsheba and, when Nathan the prophet was sent to make him face up to the truth, David knew God had heard his sin (2 Samuel 11). He is a God who 'desires truth in the inner parts' (Psalm 51:6). David was not only forgiven but God restored him and involved him again in the out-working of his redemptive purposes for Israel. Jeremiah, in regretting the day he was born and in trying to go back on his call, was not only heard by God but reinstated as his spokesman to the nation. As long as he would turn back and be true to God's calling then, said God,

> I will make you a wall to this people,
>   a fortified wall of bronze;
> they will fight against you
>   but will not overcome you,
> for I am with you
>   to rescue and save you. (Jeremiah 15:20)

Jesus lived in the daily awareness that his Father was constantly listening to him and would show him what to say and do to bring his Father's compassion, forgiveness, healing, challenge to those around him. 'Ask', 'Seek', 'Knock' he taught, for the Father knows your needs and is a generous giver. Jesus knew that his Father's attentiveness to his world was such that he heard even a sparrow fall to the ground.

Supremely, God demonstrated his listening and saving action in the death of his Son. It is the cross that shows us the lengths to which God will go in hearing the needs of his world. Jesus was obedient to the end as, stretched out on the cross, he listened to and took upon himself the full weight of the world's suffering. This is redemptive listening that not only hears but enters into and bears all our sin and pain.

God has not only spoken through his Son. What is perhaps

more important, he has listened through his Son. Christ's saving work cost him most in its speechless passivity of dereliction. It is this which gives him the right to be called the greatest listener to all suffering. It is this which gives his listening its redemptive quality.[58]

As our eyes are opened to the Father's gift of his Son, so he creates in us a desire to respond to him, listen to him, become like him, be with him in his ongoing work. For Jesus, risen and glorified, goes on listening to the world for which he died. At his Father's side he continues as great High Priest, making ceaseless prayers for us, constantly bringing to his Father the needs of the world. And God, in his amazing humility, delights to draw us into his ongoing work of redemption. We are told to come with confidence to God, following the promptings of his Spirit within us to unite our prayers with those of Jesus. Often we do not know how to pray as we ought and wonder what sense God can possibly make of what we can barely express. We are mistrustful of our inarticulate sighs and groans. Yet the Spirit helps us in our weakness. He too intercedes for us with groans that words cannot express and God 'who searches our heart knows the mind of the Spirit' (Romans 8:26,27). He knows what he will do. The wonder is that he invites us to join with him in doing it.

It is tempting to assume that prayer is at its best when we are clear and fluent . . . But prayer which is much less gratifying to our egos may often be more authentic. Times in prayer when we feel tongue-tied, . . . times when we are plagued by one distraction after another, . . . times when we experience dryness, rather than being wasted times, are often important . . . These times make us more radically aware of our need and dependence on grace. If we write off these times . . . we might be despising the gift of God, the very kind of prayer which is best for us at the time, through which God is deeply at work in us.[59]

Desmond Tutu said, on one of his visits to this country, how

much it means to Christians in South Africa that many around
the world are praying for them. He beamed from ear to ear as
he recalled how, out of the blue, he received a letter from a
Lutheran pastor in Alaska, 'I am writing to let you know that
we in the parish in Alaska are praying for you'. On another
occasion he met a hermit nun living in California. 'My day
starts at 2.30 a.m. and I pray for you', she said. He commented:

> Just as God said he would be like a wall of fire around
> Jerusalem, so we have experienced a like fire surrounding us
> – the fire of your prayers, your love, your caring. Sometimes
> it's almost a physical sensation. Don't let anyone delude you
> into believing that what you do doesn't make a difference.
> Please go on praying for us.[60]

Irina Ratushinskaya, imprisoned in a Soviet labour camp,
was saying something similar when she wrote, the day after her
release:

> Believe me, it was often thus:
> In solitary cells, on winter nights
> A sudden sense of joy and warmth
> And a resounding note of love.
> And then, unsleeping, I would know
> A-huddle by an icy wall:
> Someone is thinking of me now,
> Petitioning the Lord for me.
> My dear ones, thank you all
> Who did not falter, who believed in us!
> In the most fearful prison hour
> We probably would not have passed
> Through everything – from end to end,
> Our head held high, unbowed –
> Without your valiant hearts
> To light our path.
>   Kiev. 10 October 1986[61]

Prayer is one way in which we are called to join with Christ
in his continuing work in the world. There are many other ways

too, a few of which were described in the last chapter. Each of us is called, each of us is uniquely gifted by Christ to serve him in the world today, but that calling and gifting will be strengthened as we learn to listen.

At a large service of healing in Guildford Cathedral on the eve of Ascension Day, many people representing a wide spectrum of human need and suffering came for prayer and ministry. There was the man with cancer of the spine and a shining face, the teenager with family problems, the man who simply wanted to give thanks for a previous healing, and many others. As we quietly listened to fragments of their stories and prayed with them, I became aware of the listening God amongst us, powerful and mighty yet stooping down in tender love to hear the depths of each person. And, the following sun-filled morning, as a few of us met in the small, simple chapel at Loseley Park nearby, so we rejoiced in Christ ascended to his Father's side in heaven where he continues to listen to, hear and pray for the world for which he died. We sang:

> Still for us he intercedes, Allelujah!
> . . . Though returning to his throne
> Still he calls mankind his own, Allelujah!

All listening begins and ends in God. The God who listens in infinite compassion is the God who creates in each of us the desire to listen to him, to his world, to each other, to ourselves so that, filled with his Spirit, we might continue his work here on earth.

> Teach me to listen, Lord,
>   to those nearest me,
>   my family, my friends, my co-workers.
>   Help me to be aware that
>   no matter what words I hear,
>   the message is,
>   'Accept the person I am. Listen to me.'

Teach me to listen, Lord,
    to those far from me –
    the whisper of the hopeless,
    the plea of the forgotten,
    the cry of the anguished.

Teach me to listen, Lord,
    to myself.
    Help me to be less afraid,
    to trust the voice inside –
    in the deepest part of me.

Teach me to listen, Lord,
    for your voice –
    in busyness and in boredom,
    in certainty and in doubt,
    in noise and in silence.

Teach me, Lord, to listen.[62]

Exercises

These questions may be used for personal reflection and prayer or in a group context.

Introduction
1. Ask that God might guide you as you reflect on these three questions:

    i.   What sort of God was taught and presented to me as a child?
    ii. How do I experience God at this stage of my life?
    iii. How would I like to know, experience and relate to God?

    Listen to your feelings as well as your thoughts. Open them to God. Now read and ponder John 14:5–10, asking for the grace to know God better.

Chapter 1   Listening in the Market Place
1. As you look back over the last few days, do you sense you have heard God in the midst of your daily affairs? In what ways?
2. As you begin a new day, open yourself to God asking him to create in you a still centre where, during the pressures of the day, you can talk and listen to him.
3. Take into your day a Bible verse that has struck you – you may want to write it out on a small card – and, at different points in the day, recall the words and let them nurture you.

Chapter 2   Listening in the Desert
1. Try including a 'little solitude' in an ordinary working day. This may be after the children have gone to school or in the lunch-hour or evening. Read slowly a few verses from a Psalm or another Bible passage. Or simply be still, opening yourself to the God who loves you.
2. Consider, individually or as a group, the possibility of an evening or part of a day for a mini-retreat. Try to go to a

quiet place away from your home or work surroundings. Joyce Huggett, *Open to God*, and Martin Smith, *The Word is Very Near You*, provide helpful ideas as to how to use the time.

3. Plan a listening walk in a garden, park, countryside. Before going, read Psalm 8 slowly, opening your senses to God – eyes, ears, touch, smell, taste – and ask him to meet you in his creation. As you set out, slow down and take a few deep breaths. Feel the ground under your feet, the air on your skin. Listen to the sounds around you. Touch a tree, the grass, a flower. Be aware of your feelings. Look at things closely and ask yourself,

   — what attracts me about this?
   — is God wanting to speak to me?

4. For a group listening to God, use a Bible passage (e.g. Psalm 27, Isaiah 55, John 15:1-7, Philippians 2:1-11).

   — if possible have seats arranged in a circle.
   — invite people to relax and open themselves to God.
   — the group leader asks Christ, the living Word, to be in the midst and for the Holy Spirit to lead.
   — one of the group reads out the passage, then allow a few minutes of silence for reflection.
   — the leader invites people to share, without comment, a word or phrase that has struck them. It doesn't matter if some choose the same verse. Allow pauses between each contribution.
   — another person re-reads the passage. Allow time for silent reflection again.
   — the leader invites any who would like to, to share briefly how a verse from the passage has spoken personally – perhaps bringing comfort, challenge, direction, insight etc.
   — a third person re-reads the passage with silence following.

— the group is invited to offer personal thanksgivings and prayers to God.

Chapter 3 Discerning God's Voice

1. Can you think of an occasion when you sensed God was speaking to you and time and events confirmed this?

   Can you think of another occasion when you sensed God was speaking to you but time and events showed you it was not his voice?

   What did you learn through this? Be aware of your feelings as well as your thoughts.

2. Reflect on some key occasions in your life when you heard God – perhaps in guidance, encouragement, challenge, etc., through the Bible, another person, creation, an inner voice, music etc. – and thank him.

3. In what ways have you, as a church, listened to and heard God over particular issues? Is there sufficient opportunity to grow in listening to God together and discerning his voice? (e.g. leadership team, P.C.C., house groups, etc.) See pages 164–5.

4. Listening to God in small groups.

   In groups of four:

   (a) in turn *share* a situation you are currently praying for or a concern you have.

   The others simply listen without asking questions.

   (b) the group wait in silence before God and *listen* concerning the situation or person.

   (c) if any is given a word, insight, Bible verse, picture, *speak* it out briefly, without discussion. The person who shared will usually have the insight to sift out what has been said. If nothing is given, stay in silence.

   (d) one person should then *pray*, committing the situation or person to God.

   Move on to the next person.

   N.B. discourage discussion in the group.

   Don't press anyone to share or pray aloud if they would rather not.

Chapter 4   Listening and Responding
1. Reflect on times when you (personally or as a church)
    heard God and responded to him in a particular way (e.g.
    meeting a local need, visiting etc.). What was the outcome?
    Be aware of your feelings as you reflect.
2. Can you think of any ways in which God has given you
    direction (personally or as a church) and you have not
    acted on it? Is he saying anything to you now about that?
    Again, be aware of feelings as well as thoughts that come
    to you.

Chapter 5_ A Listening God
1. Individually or as a group, find other biblical examples of
    people becoming aware that God listens to and hears them.
    You might like to look at Hannah (1 Samuel 1:20) and
    David (Psalm 5:3) and find others.
2. Can you think of particular occasions recently when you
    sensed God listening to and hearing you?
3. 'We are mistrustful of our inarticulate sighs and groans.'
    'It is tempting to assume that prayer is at its best where
    we are clear and fluent.'
    Reflect on or discuss these statements. Do we allow for
    the 'sighs and groans' as well as the 'clear and fluent', both
    in our personal and corporate praying? (e.g. how might
    this affect a group meeting for prayer?)

References

1. Donald Coggan, *The Sacrament of the Word* (Collins Fount, 1987), pp. 31, 32.
2. Lesslie Newbigin, lecture given at the Churches' Council of Health and Healing Conference, 1988 and printed in the Journal of the Institute of Religion and Medicine (vol. 4, no. 2, 1988).
3. Gerard Hughes SJ, *God of Surprises* (DLT, 1985), p. 34.
4. *ibid.*, p. 36.
5. Sheila Cassidy, *Prayer for Pilgrims* (Collins Fount, 1980) p. 87.
6. Esther de Waal, *Living with Contradiction* (Collins Fount, 1989), p. 115.
7. Sister Margaret Magdalen CSMV, *Jesus – Man of Prayer* (Hodder & Stoughton, 1987), p. 21.
8. Trans. E. M. Blaiklock, Brother Lawrence, *The Practice of the Presence of God* (Hodder & Stoughton, 1981), p. 45.
9. Esther de Waal, *Seeking God* (Collins Fount, 1984), p. 105.
10. Henri Nouwen, *Reaching Out* (Collins, 1976), p. 52.
11. Donald Coggan, *op. cit.*, p. 32.
12. Sue Monk Kidd, *God's Joyful Surprise* (Hodder & Stoughton, 1990), p. 117.
13. Thomas R. Kelly, *A Testament of Devotion*, quoted by Richard Foster, *Celebration of Discipline*, p. 40.
14. Brother Lawrence, *op. cit.*, p. 41.
15. Henri Nouwen, *The Way of the Heart* (DLT, 1981), pp. 25,26.
16. Henri Nouwen, *Out of Solitude* (Ave Maria Press, 1974), pp. 14,15.
17. Richard Foster, *op. cit.*, p. 93.
18. Sue Monk Kidd, *op. cit.*, p. 88.
19. Joyce Huggett, *Open to God* (Hodder & Stoughton, 1989), p. 81.

20. See Joyce Huggett, *ibid*. Also John Pearce, *Advance by Retreat* (Grove Books, 1989). For group ideas see Graham Pigott, *Helpful Habits* (Grove Books, 1989).

21. Maria Boulding, *The Coming of God* (SPCK, 1982), p. 7.

22. Sue Monk Kidd, *op. cit.*, p. 107. -

23. Philip Sheldrake, *Images of Holiness* (DLT, 1987), p. 92.

24. Mother Teresa, *In the Silence of the Heart* (SPCK, 1983), p. 19.

25. Henri Nouwen, *The Way of the Heart*, p. 30.

26. Thomas Merton, *No Man is an Island* (Burns & Oates, 1955), p. 61.

27. Ed. John Macquarrie, *A Dictionary of Christian Ethics* (SCM Press), p. 158.

28. Douglas McBain, *Eyes that See* (Marshall Pickering, 1986), p. 1.

29. John Carroll Futrell SJ, *Ignatian Discernment* (Studies in the Spirituality of Jesuits, vol. II, April 1970, no. 2).

30. Douglas McBain, *op. cit.*, p. 5.

31. David Lonsdale SJ, *Eyes to See, Ears to Hear* (DLT, 1990), p. 69.

32. John Powell SJ, *He Touched Me* (Argus Communications, 1974), p. 79.

33. Sister Margaret Magdalen CSMV, *op. cit.*, p. 96.

34. Douglas McBain, *op. cit.*, p. 74. The whole of his chapter on Discernment and Scripture is well worth reading.

35. Thomas M. Green SJ, *Weeds Among the Wheat* (Ave Maria Press, 1984), p. 64.

36. W. A. Barry and W. J. Connolly, *The Practice of Spiritual Direction* (Seabury Press, 1983), p. 108.

37. Thomas Green SJ, *op. cit.*, p. 202.

38. For further insight into the Ignatian understanding of discernment, see Gerard Hughes SJ, *op. cit.*, ch. 8 and David Lonsdale SJ, *op. cit.*, ch. 4.

39. John R. Sheets SJ, *The Four Moments of Prayer, in Notes on the Spiritual Exercises of St Ignatius of Loyola* (ed. David Fleming SJ, 1983), p. 169.

40. John Gunstone, *The Charismatic Prayer Group* (Hodder Christian Paperbacks), p. 99.
41. *ibid.*, p. 100.
42. David Lonsdale sj, *op. cit.*, p. 81.
43. Douglas McBain, *op. cit.*, p. 147.
44. Mother Teresa, *op. cit.*, p. 1.
45. Harry Williams cr, *The Joy of God* (Mitchell Beazley, 1979), p. 109.
46. Esther de Waal, *Seeking God*, pp. 43,44.
47. Thomas A. Smail, *The Forgotten Father* (Hodder & Stoughton, 1980), p. 71.
48. *ibid.*, p. 37.
49. Quoted in Esther de Waal, *Seeking God*, p. 49.
50. Philip Sheldrake, *op. cit.*, p. 94.
51. Neville Cryer, *Michel Quoist: a Biography* (Hodder & Stoughton, 1977), p. 53.
52. Philip Sheldrake, *op. cit.*, p. 96.
53. Clarry Hendrickse, *One Inner City Church and Lay Ministry* (Grove Books, 1983), p. 3.
54. *ibid.*, pp. 17–18.
55. *ibid.*, p. 20.
56. John V. Taylor, *Kingdom Come* (SCM Press, 1989), p. 70.
57. Collect for Easter 5, *Alternative Service Book* (Oxford University Press, 1980), p. 622.
58. Frank Lake, *Listening and Responding* (a pamphlet produced by the Clinical Theology Association), p. 13.
59. Martin Smith, *The Word is Very Near You* (DLT, 1990), p. 23.
60. Desmond Tutu, from an address in St Albans Abbey, 1988.
61. Irina Ratushinskaya, 'Believe Me', from *Pencil Letter* (Bloodaxe Books, 1988).
62. John Veltri sj, *Orientations Vol. 1* (Loyola House, Guelph, Ontario, Canada, 1979), p. 46.